FOREIGN EXCHANGE
DEALER'S HANDBOOK

To
Mary, Jonathan, Fiona and Jeremy

FOREIGN EXCHANGE DEALER'S HANDBOOK

RAYMOND G F CONINX

Director, Tullett & Riley (Financial Services) Company Ltd

WOODHEAD-FAULKNER
CAMBRIDGE

Woodhead-Faulkner Ltd
17 Market Street
Cambridge CB2 3PA

First published 1982

© Raymond G F Coninx 1982

ISBN 0 85941 152 4

Designed by Geoff Green

Typeset by Bookens, Saffron Walden, Essex
Printed in Great Britain by The Thetford Press Ltd,
Thetford, Norfolk

PREFACE

The question 'Is foreign exchange dealing an art or a science (or neither)?' would provide a solid topic for protracted debate. I must confess that I would tend to side with the view that it is neither. Too many dealing decisions are made intuitively. The dealer is presented with an opportunity to trade and he either makes a price or forgoes the possibility of assisting a valuable customer or correspondent bank. The situation is completely different when the operator has the time and the inclination to judge the merits of a proposal. Even then it is often a case of a 'for better or for worse', toss of a coin decision.

In my previous book *Foreign Exchange Today* I attempted to give an introduction to this subject. It was intended for the beginner with little or no knowledge of currency dealing. By familiarizing himself with the origin, recent history and some of the techniques employed by the professional traders, the neophyte then should have been able to build on that elementary knowledge by gaining experience in the real world.

Over the many years I spent in dealing rooms coping with the problems raised by customers and fellow officers, I would have appreciated having a handy reference book at my disposal. However, most of the textbooks on foreign exchange stop short at being straight reference books and quite often do not contain sufficient mathematical information to be of real use in everyday life.

It is the intricacies of such subjects as interest arbitrage, compound interest, discount, and discount to yield which at times cloud the minds of the professional dealers. I hope that this manual will ease their mental deliberations and not only speed up their 'response times' but also improve the accuracy of their calculations.

Although this manual is dedicated almost in its entirety to the mathematics applicable to foreign exchange and money dealing, this does not mean that the reader requires more than an elementary knowledge of financial arithmetic. Even for a professional there will always be occasions when easy reference to the appropriate formula will save time and expense.

The gradual growth of the currency markets since the Second World War is mainly responsible for the lack of formal training of young dealers coming into the profession. The haphazard nature of learning the techniques and arithmetic of dealing, which is usually left to the whims of the Chief Dealer, can leave gaps in the know-how of the trader. Furthermore, by not undergoing a formalized professional education in his chosen career, the dealer may well adopt practices and reasoning which, to say the least, are misguided, if not totally incorrect, when applied to real trading situations. Fortunately for the new entrant a number of studies and books have been published in recent years on the subject of foreign exchange which have introduced scientific approaches to the basically subjective world of currency dealing.

After all the basics of foreign exchange dealing are fairly simple. A dealer or customer buys one currency in exchange for another, and one of these currencies may be his own. This operation requires no mathematical genius, as simple multiplication or division is the sum total of the arithmetical knowledge required. It is when the interlocking activities of deposit dealing and interest arbitrage intrude on this simplicity that the mathematical knowledge needed to establish the viability of transactions increases exponentially. Further complications are added when interest arbitrage transactions are entered into for periods of longer than one year.

Continuing high levels of inflation and concomitant rates of interest in many countries have contributed to the necessity of greater awareness of such tools as compound interest formulas. The high interest rate levels are exacerbated by wide interest rate differentials between countries. Obviously, when the interest differential between two countries amounts to only 1 per cent – for instance, 7 per cent and 8 per cent respectively – this will lead to smaller distortions than if they differ by 5 per cent – let us say, 5 per cent and 10 per cent. Points like these will be discussed in detail in the various chapters on interest arbitrage and forward dealing.

It is, of course, impossible to produce a handbook which covers every possible variation of exchange and deposit dealing. Most of the time when an operator is presented with a convoluted proposition he will have to break it down into its component parts. Is it a foreign exchange transaction, a deposit deal or a mixture of both? Once he has divided the proposition into manageable segments, he can begin to apply his knowledge and experience. He may then find that he has to apply the compound interest or discount to yield formula, and in many instances he may have to use a variety of formulas to arrive at a satisfactory conclusion. Financial transactions for periods in excess of one year bring special problems in their wake. They are never simple unless every exposure aspect can be squared away and even then some small risk areas may remain uncovered. It is then that the trader shows his analytical powers. He may have to make assumptions based on probable outcomes if certain conditions are fulfilled.

Computers, sophisticated pocket calculators and other space-age gadgetry have taken some of the hard 'slog' out of the arithmetic applied in the dealing room. On the other hand, electronic equipment can only be employed to its fullest advantage if the operator knows how to interpret data and how to assess information. Without adequate input, the output is going to be valueless. As the saying goes, 'garbage in, garbage out'. Naturally, in view of the mathematical aids available to all dealers, it seems unnecessary to include an explanation of long division or multiplication in this book. It is taken for granted that the reader will be sufficiently apprised of these elementary routines.

Not all dealing rooms are fully computerized and many problems have still to be worked out by the dealer. He may not have the software at his disposal that will do the calculating for him and it is especially for these individuals that this handbook was written.

Although the terminology used in the market is fairly standardized, there are still a number of 'in-house' expressions which are meaningless when mentioned to an outsider. These differences of phraseology are caused by the nationality of a bank and the type of banking business it specializes in. For this reason the first section of most chapters is devoted to essential terminology to ensure that the reader understands the reference and also to improve readability, as otherwise, the same description would have to be used time and again.

The equations and formulas applied in the book to solve problems are listed in the Appendix for easy reference. Wherever it makes sense, the formulas will be simplified to their most elementary form, although it cannot be emphasized enough that shortcuts can lead to mistakes and that sometimes it is better to go the 'long route', particularly if a transaction happens infrequently and the dealer is 'a bit stale'. Regular revision of complicated brain-twisters will also ensure that formulas stay fresh in the operator's mind, so that when a problem arises he can recall which formula is most appropriate.

Although many pamphlets are issued by secondary market traders on certificates of deposit computations they are usually kept by the deposit dealers and out of reach of the foreign exchange people. In these days of overlapping deposit and foreign exchange activities, it is absolutely essential that all dealers, whether specializing in foreign exchange or currency deposits, have a basic grounding in, and have access to, the mathematics of finance in general.

I have devoted a short chapter to financial futures, as the role of the exchanges is becoming more important in the present state of market uncertainty. As the subject is a complex one and deserves a whole volume to itself, the chapter will only set out the basic advantages and some of the drawbacks and an introduction to the dealing and arithmetical techniques employed by professional traders in financial futures.

CONTENTS

1

EXCHANGE RATES

Definition

The exchange rate is the price at which a currency can be bought or sold in terms of another. This price can be the result of supply and demand for the currency in the open, unrestricted market, or, at the other extreme, firmly fixed by edict of a government or its monetary authority, usually the central bank.

But, most of the time the value of currencies is decided by the interaction of the free market forces playing their role, alleviated by the intervention of the monetary authorities to ensure their currencies do not depreciate or appreciate excessively. The latter form of fixing currency exchange rates is sometimes called a 'dirty float'. Why it deserves this derogatory modifier is not quite clear, as monetary authorities would not be doing their duty if they did not intervene in the market place to smooth out excessive price movements, that is, unless we ascribe a completely passive function to monetary authorities, *i.e.* taking away their authority.

Types of Exchange Rates

Direct Quotations

In most countries the internal exchange rates are expressed in units of the national currency. This is the so-called direct quotation system. For instance, in West Germany one US dollar will be worth x units of Deutsche Marks and in New York, one Deutsche Mark will be worth x cents (or dollars if the Deutsche Mark appreciated considerably). Lately there has been a tendency among professional traders in the United States foreign exchange market to deal on an indirect basis with the outside world and among themselves.

Indirect Quotations

The United Kingdom is one of the few places applying the indirect quotation system. As mentioned above, New York is another centre which finds it preferable to adopt a system valuing the national unit of account rather than the foreign one. In London, the US dollar will be quoted as x units of dollars worth one pound sterling. In other words, the indirect quotation system values the pound or the dollar in terms of other currencies (even when they are the home currencies).

But whatever system is employed, when two cross border interests wish to transact foreign currency business, one of them will have to apply an indirect quotation when dealing in each other's currencies.

Cross Rates

An exchange rate is called a cross rate when the national currency is not party to the transaction. A London bank buying or selling Deutsche Marks against US dollars is obviously using a cross rate. For dealings in the international market, cross rates with US dollars are often used, as the US dollar is not only the world's main reserve currency, but also provides the base currency for most exchange transactions. For instance, it is easier for a buyer of French francs against Deutsche Marks to acquire the French francs against dollars and then to buy the dollars against Deutsche Marks, rather than to try to obtain a competitive French franc/Deutsche Mark quotation. Naturally, there are banks providing French franc/Deutsche Mark rates (or vice versa) in Paris and Frankfurt, but this kind of specialist service to a limited market may include a cost element in the pricing.

Of course, if a buyer of French francs against Deutsche Marks could execute the purchase without going through the US dollar, and given there was no extra cost involved, he would be foolish not to do so. Not only would he save the execution costs of two transactions compared to one, but he would also avoid an exposure risk, as it is well-nigh impossible to synchronize two exchange operations with different parties. There will also be a slight risk that the rates may move before both deals have been finalized, and it may happen that the amounts are too large for one of the counterparties, thus possibly necessitating three or four deals instead of two. The intention to realize a profit or minimize a loss situation should always be paramount in a dealer's mind, consequently, the fewer transactions necessary to reach a satisfactory conclusion the better.

Forward Rates

While the exchange rate is also the spot rate for a currency (*see* Chapter 2) and the numeraire for the national currency, the forward rate is sometimes looked upon as the true indicator of what value a currency should have at a particular time in the future. Or at least, the forward rate should provide an approximation and a strong indication of the direction of a future exchange rate. It is doubtful, however, whether the trend or the future are clearly defined in a forward rate. Most times, forward rates show the interest differentials operative in the countries of the currencies involved in an exchange operation.

It must be said though, that forward rates are of more value to the commercial user of the market than the spot rates. The forward rates are the true indicators of what prices are appropriate for imports and exports of services and goods, in view of the time-lag between negotiation, execution and delivery.

It is debatable whether forward rates start from the day after spot onwards, or seven days forward or even one month. This is a question of preference and is usually strongly influenced by the internal accounting standards of an organization, or those laid down by official bodies. For official reporting purposes, the spot rate is commonly the one applied for the same day. A bank closing its books on a particular day, let us say a Monday, would consider that Monday as being the spot date and the next day (Tuesday) and all the following days would simply be counted as forwards. This is a very logical attitude, as positions actually processed over the books of foreign contacts on that day are irreversible, whereas positions taken for the following and ensuing days can, in theory at least, still be reversed (matched).

Forward rates are quoted for the major currencies up to five years' delivery, sometimes longer, and for others up to one year or for shorter periods, depending on the attitude taken by the appropriate monetary authority or the depth of the interbank market in these currencies. The longer the maturity the more difficult it becomes to obtain competitive dealing rates. Quotations may be made, but frequently they just form a basis for discussion. As the number of market-makers declines rapidly the longer the maturity, it is normal to find that even in major currencies like sterling, only one market-maker is to be found in a particular period over one year at any one time. An interested party is then very much limited to negotiating a price with the longer-term market-maker. Whether he is successful will depend on having a good credit rating and his not having utilized the internal limit of the quoting bank. It pays to be miserly with long-term contracts, as it can prove difficult to find more than one counterparty over a period of time. For those considering offering specialist services in longer than one year periods, they must make sure that there are sufficient numbers of other participants in the time segment or else they must be prepared to run risks for long periods of time without being able to 'unload' their positions.

Forward exchange rates are calculated in the same way as spot rates. Conversion techniques are the same, once the rate has been established. As will be seen in the chapters on outright forward rates and interest arbitrage (*see* Chapters 3 and 5), it is not so much the actual rate that creates problems, it is how to 'concoct' one or to check its accuracy that necessitates a logical mind.

2

SPOT RATES

Definition

The spot rate for a currency is the price quoted for the nearest standard settlement day for the purchase or sale of this currency against another one. The spot rate, whether floating freely or fixed by the authorities, reflects the external value of a currency at the time of dealing. For some currencies there may be an internal and external value, but as this usually applies to controlled exchange activities, it is really the rate for normal commercial transactions, mostly imports and exports of goods and services, that is the exchange and spot rate.

The Effects of Exchange Controls on National Exchange Markets

Foreign currency operators in countries with rigid exchange controls have little opportunity to exercise their skills. In some countries the authorities fix the exact buying and selling rates periodically, even daily, in which case foreign exchange dealing is practically non-existent, unless there is a gap in the regulations permitting some arbitrage transactions between different currency bands.

When there are no (or practically no) exchange controls, the development and depth of the exchange market is a question of the willingness of the domestic banks to take views and to back these up with positions. Naturally, the size and volume of a domestic market in foreign currencies is limited by the size of the country, population figures, the state of the economy and the number of participants in the market. Obviously, in a small country with only a few banks and a limited money supply, a currency market against the national unit of account is very restricted and a comprehensive exchange market is unlikely to develop.

A lack of exchange controls also means that the banks operating in the foreign exchange market of a country will be responsible to ensure prudent dealing by imposing limitations. However, instead of having exchange controls, the central bank or monetary authority may inhibit the freedom of the dealers by setting capital and other ratios on the positions they are allowed to carry for a limited period.

The Role of Market-makers

In countries where relative freedom exists, it will be the market-makers who set the rates depending on supply and demand or in the anticipation of supply or demand. Market-makers are found mainly among the very large banks and the multinational and large national companies. Passive users of the market contribute little to its development, although, if they have substantial amounts to transact, their activities may force the professionals to adjust the open market rates.

Market-making, of course, does not take place only in foreign currencies against the national one, it can also apply to providing firm quotations for one foreign currency against another without the national currency being involved. On the whole, the market-making in a currency takes place primarily in the country of a currency. The main market-makers in Deutsche Marks will be found in West Germany and for Swiss francs in Switzerland. The exception might be in the main reserve currencies, the US dollar in particular, as the whole world uses the dollar as the basis for foreign exchange transactions. Consequently, market-making in US dollars is not necessarily confined to New York, unless the Federal Reserve Bank is acting as a catalyst to protect the value of the dollar. Except in the latter case, the market for US dollars will be in Frankfurt, or London, or wherever the national currency of a country is dealt against the dollar. The reason for this phenomenon is simply that a reserve currency is held by many more participants and is easier to acquire or to dispose of than a non-reserve currency in the deposit markets. Although over the last two decades the Deutsche Mark has become one of the strongest currencies in the world, it has never assumed the status of reserve currency in the true sense of the word. Deutsche Marks are frequently held for purely speculative purposes, and holders dispose of them as soon as a clear profit is realizable.

When discussing the strength or weakness of a currency, new entrants must be careful with the use of terminology. This includes such simple things as knowing, for example, that when a New York operator talks about the weakness of a currency he may be talking about Deutsche Marks or sterling but not necessarily about his own national money the dollar.

A market-maker will quote buying and selling rates in the currencies in which he claims expertise. Very few banks cover all the currencies in the world, though the large national banks – like the clearing banks in the United Kingdom – will have to provide a comprehensive range of quotations to their commercial customers. Frequently the more exotic currencies will be handled by service departments rather than by the dealing rooms. In any case, the exotic currencies are quite often those of countries where there is no developed exchange market or where restrictions prohibit the free in- or outflow of foreign currencies. Usually these regulations will be more concerned with outflows than inflows, of course. If they cannot help their customers on a direct basis then the banks, whether large or small, will use their branch or correspondent networks to process a payment or receipt in another currency.

Bidding and Offering

In foreign exchange parlance buying and selling rates are often referred to as *bid* and *offered* prices or rates. And many times, less obvious expressions to show a buying or selling interest will be uttered by professionals but, on the whole, it is preferable to make use of clear, succinct language and to avoid jargon. The terms bid, offer, buying and selling are confusing enough in themselves, as they can only be applied when it is known who is doing the bidding or offering.

The professional operator, whether an active market-maker or not, will in most instances quote buying and selling rates for some of the major currencies. Currently, active dealing rooms will have expertise in Deutsche Marks, sterling, the ubiquitous US dollar and possibly in a few other major currencies.

A dealer in Frankfurt, for instance, is almost bound to quote the US dollar against Deutsche Marks. Another bank approaching this dealer in Frankfurt for his quotations may be told:

Bid	*Offer*
DM2.0000	DM2.0005 (shortened to 00–25)

The 2.00 would be referred to as the *big figure*, and unless the US dollar appreciated or depreciated to 2.01 or 1.99, no other mention would be made other than 00–25 on 40–60 (*i.e.* 2.0000–2.0025 or 2.0040–2.0060). Sometimes when a dealer is quoted a rate in points 00–25 and the market has been extremely volatile, he may request 'what is the big figure?' to be told 5, 7, 4 or whatever, in this case, 2.04, 2.05, but he would then have to make sure that the value had not gone below 2.00, *i.e.* 1.94–1.95, etc.

In other words, the operator in West Germany expresses a willingness to buy dollars at DM2.0000 (he is bidding for US dollars) and to sell the North American currency at DM2.0005. If the market in US dollars were static at the time, the dealer in Frankfurt would hope that he could get an even number of buyers and sellers or at least that the total amount of his 'boughts' would match his 'solds'. If he happened to realize that dream he would make a profit of DM0.0005 for each dollar sold matched by a purchase or vice versa.

Example 2.1

Putting the quotations into a more practical context, a purchase of US$1,000,000 at a cost of DM2,000,000 which was then sold at

DM2,000,500 would produce a profit of DM500. A considerable sum for a seemingly straightforward operation unless one takes into account that the back-office work and the cost of transmitting money will erode most of the profit margin, if not all of the profit margin.

To break even the dealer would have to turn over many deals of US$1,000,000 or deal in larger amounts. In static markets it is very difficult for dealing rooms to generate large profits – conversely, large losses do not arise either. That is why dealers prefer to operate in fluctuating markets, as these offer opportunities for substantial margins between buying and selling. In that case it is more a question of taking calculated risks (euphemism for speculation) than trading in and out of a currency.

It would be doubtful if the German dealer in this example would have continued to quote DM2.0000–2.0005 unless he were absolutely certain that his rates were among the best in the market. In a real life situation the amount might have had to be larger than US$1,000,000, which might have encouraged him to change his quotation to 1.9999–2.0004 or, if more sellers of dollars had shown up at DM2.0000, he could have adjusted his prices to DM1.9996–2.0001. If this were not sufficient to stop the selling interest and he became uncomfortable with the whole situation, he might have quoted DM1.9995–2.0000 or even a quotation at which he would be certain to make a loss if a buyer of dollars 'hit' him at his price.

But this time good fortune favoured the Frankfurt dealer and he generated a clear profit; however, in percentage terms before costs an insignificant profit of $(0.0005 \times 100) \div 2.0000 = 0.025$ per cent was realized when looked at as the profit on the purchase of US$1,000,000, but was only 0.0125 per cent when the total volume (US$2,000,000) is taken into account. When this percentage profit margin is annualized the picture looks less gloomy and if the same result could be obtained throughout the year it would produce a better profit margin than normally obtained on commercial loans. Naturally, the volume would have to be enormous and if these results could be obtained on larger transactions it would also help to cut the processing costs.

The Effects of Quotation Systems

We used the example of a West German bank buying and selling US dollars priced in Deutsche Marks. Thus, the value of the US dollar is clear to any buyer or seller of the currencies. This is usually referred to as the direct quotation system (*see* Chapter 1, page 1). The national currency is used to denote the value of a foreign unit (or appropriate round amount of units). There are some advantages inherent in direct quotations, the main one being that to convert the cost of a given amount of US dollars into Deutsche Marks only requires simple multiplication.

A US bank in New York using the same quotation of DM2.0000–05 would be using the indirect quotation system. But more and more this is becoming the norm in reserve currency countries. That is also why the London market still applies the indirect quotation system even in the local market. In other words, the exchange rates state the value of one pound in terms of the foreign currency.

However, as the prevailing tendency favours round amounts of US dollars and pounds sterling, the operators in the United States and the United Kingdom are usually left with oddments of foreign currency, whereas the operators in direct quotation countries dealing in round amounts of the foreign currency immediately realize profits and losses in terms of their national currency, their own unit of account.

The old maxim 'buy high, sell low', which was often quoted as the guiding principle for dealers under the indirect dealing system of London when sterling was the major reserve currency, is unfashionable now. When sterling provided the base currency it made sense to acquire as many foreign currency units for the cost of one pound and to sell as few as possible in return for a pound. These days when the direct dealing approach is more widely practiced, it is more a question of 'buying low and selling high'. The latter statement can now be applied in the London market, as there is a tendency to buy and sell sterling in round amounts rather than the foreign currency, with the exception of contracts entered into with UK commercial interests.

In reality, it makes little difference whether the direct or indirect system is used, as dealers quickly adjust to the change in emphasis.

Example 2.2

    If Incorporated Inc. in New York wish to acquire sterling and contact a New York bank they may be quoted the figures 2.2510–15 and, if these rates prove to be as competitive or no worse than the rates quoted by other banks, Incorporated Inc. might buy, let us say, £1,000,000 at 2.2515. The bank is selling high and the customer is buying high.

    The maxim holds true in its updated form only when it refers to the actions of a market-maker. To the user of the market it only means that the best rate should be obtained from a suitable source. On the spot date the New York bank will pay the customer £1,000,000 in London and receive in compensation US\$2,251,500. Of course, Incorporated Inc. could have decided that a better rate was obtainable from a London bank. If some London bank keen to attract business from a multinational corporation in the USA had quoted 2.2511–14, naturally, Incorporated Inc. would have acquired the sterling in London, in the process saving US\$100 before deducting the cost of the telex or telephone communications.

Commercial customers are less likely to buy or sell in round amounts unless they are engaging in interest arbitrage. For instance, if a New York company wishes to take advantage of higher interest rates in the UK, it converts an odd amount of dollars into a round amount of sterling. However, most of the time, commercial customers will come to the market to cover odd amounts, either buying or selling the proceeds of an export or import transaction and these rarely add up to nice marketable sums. An export company in the United Kingdom may wish to sell US$131,555, which in dealing terms is a very small amount and difficult, if not impossible, to unwind in the interbank market. Very likely the customer wanting to acquire or dispose of such a small amount will not obtain a prime rate, as the bank has to accumulate many of these small amounts before it becomes worthwhile to cover the exposure in the market.

Fortunately, the same inhibitions do not prevail in the more exotic or smaller currencies. Banks will not hesitate to undo small positions in non-market currencies to get rid of unwanted exposures, as it is most unlikely that they would build up sufficient volume in the course of a dealing day. The usual course then is to contact a bank in the country of the currency and to explain that the contacting bank has to dispose of or acquire a small amount. The market-maker will then widen the quotation or, in some instances, may even do the small amount at the going market rates in order to retain the custom.

The activities of commercial customers and small correspondents, however, mar the positions of the dealers. Some commercial activities are not even handled in the dealing room and it is often only the following day that the dealers will be informed that other departments have bought or sold *x* amount of a foreign currency, that is, if the amount is worth reporting. These days with computerization going ahead, more and more other departments input their small dealing activities straight into the overall foreign exchange positions, making it easier for the traders to keep track of the banks' real exposures in foreign currencies.

As stated before, the main difference between the direct and indirect quotation systems is in the calculations necessary to convert a foreign currency amount into the national one.

Example 2.3

A customer buying US$1,000,000 against Deutsche Marks at 2.0005 will only have to multiply, and with a round amount like $1,000,000, he will not need the assistance of a calculator.

On the other hand, a customer in the UK buying US$1,000,000 at 2.2520 will find it a little more difficult to compute the required sterling equivalent which will have to be paid to his bankers on the spot date. He will have to divide US$1,000,000 by 2.2520 to come up with £444,049.73.

Most calculators take care of the rounding-off process leaving the appropriate two digits after the decimal points. It almost seems superfluous to clarify that when the result of an exchange conversion shows 0.005 in the third place after the decimal point, the 0.005 is rounded up to 0.01 and anything lower than 0.005 is rounded down. For instance, if the result showed 0.0549, then rounding off would bring it back to 0.05 whereas 0.055 would produce 0.06.

Transactions in Third Currencies

Straightforward exchange rates do not on the whole create problems for the dealers. They are quite used to moving their quotations up or down depending on what view they take of market trends or how they wish to handle their existing positions. The same considerations do not apply when a quotation has to be manufactured out of a third currency. As the US dollar is the base currency for most transactions, even against the national currencies, competitive quotations for a minor currency against another one or even against a major currency are not easily obtained. Most of the wheeling and dealing is in sterling/dollars; dollars/Deutsche Marks; dollars/Swiss francs, etc. When a dealer or a customer wants a realistic price for French francs against Belgian francs or against Deutsche Marks, he may find that there are not many specialists in the market giving this kind of service. And worse still, they may charge hidden fees in the rates for offering these facilities. The only way the interested party can then check the accuracy of the quotation is to go through the two dollar/currency quotations to arrive at the currency/currency rate.

Example 2.4

One pound sterling	US$2.2510–15
One US dollar	DM2.0000–05

The first rate states the value of one pound in dollar terms and the second the value of one dollar in Deutsche Mark terms. Although it may have become second nature, the dealer will reason that if he wishes to acquire Deutsche Marks against sterling he will first of all have to buy dollars against sterling at 2.2510 and then with the dollars buy Deutsche Marks at a rate of 2.0000. Thus, the rate at which he can obtain Deutsche Marks against sterling is arrived at by multiplying 2.2510 by 2.0000 = 4.502 and conversely, he can dispose of Deutsche Marks at 2.2515 × 2.0005 = 4.504125. It is highly unlikely that a market quotation for Deutsche Marks against sterling would be as accurate as this, and 4.5020–4.5045 would be more realistic. If the operator found a better rate in the market for a straight sterling/Deutsche Mark transaction, let us say, 4.5025, then he would not hesitate to buy the currency at this rate against sterling. It would mean that fewer settlements would have to be made, and the risk of making mistakes either in-house or by one of the intermediaries to the transaction lessened.

Use of Cross Rates

Sometimes, when a dealer has a very large amount to cover and this proves difficult to execute in one deal at one exchange rate, the use of the so-called cross rates – not involving the national currency – can spread the risk and keep the rates competitive. Also, it is to the advantage of a trader who has to cover a substantial amount, to keep the market guessing as to its magnitude and direction. This may apply just as much to a normal dollar currency transaction where a quick series of sales, or purchases, of relatively modest amounts with a number of banks may leave the market undisturbed. The disadvantage of this approach is that some of the other parties may feel slighted if they find out that their contact has spoilt the market for them. The first buyer or seller in the chain who gets to know that this customer has executed similar transactions with other parties at more advantageous terms and has left him 'sitting' on his position, might be less than happy with this approach. Next time round he may feel inclined to request his customer – in suitable language – to take his business elsewhere. He might even feel inclined to trade the same way as his ex-customer, that is, if he is reasonably certain of the latter's intentions.

Awareness of costs and of limiting the number of transactions necessary to reach a satisfactory conclusion are the two considerations which should be paramount in the minds of the dealers, next to the primary aim of making profits, of course.

When dealers in two centres operate in each other's currencies one of the contractants will have to deal on an indirect basis. To establish that the rate for his own national currency in the foreign market is commensurate with the reciprocal rate in the domestic market is a simple computation.

Example 2.5

If the Danish Kroner is quoted in Paris as Dkr100 equal Ffr75, then the reciprocal rate in Copenhagen for 100 French francs should be:

$$\frac{100}{75} \times 100 = \text{Dkr}133.33; \text{ as Dkr}100 = \text{Ffr}75 \text{ then:}$$

$$\text{Ffr}75 \times \frac{133.33}{100} = \text{Dkr}99.9975$$

or, rounded up, Dkr100.

In a similar fashion, if one US dollar is worth DM2.00, then a dealer in the United States quoting in dollar terms might quote:

$$\frac{1.00}{2.00} = US\$0.50$$

for one Deutsche Mark.

Care must be taken however when a rate is converted into a reciprocal price. Whereas it is beneficial to buy low when acquiring Danish Kroner in Paris, when reversing the rate for use in Copenhagen the opposite applies. The French franc should then be sold at the highest possible rate. Mistakes sometimes occur when quoting customers in the currency of their preference. Dealers at times find it difficult to adjust to the new situation, especially when they have quoted the rates in one fashion and then have to change the quotation to comply with a customer's preference.

Errors can also occur when two dollar/currency rates are used to produce currency/currency rates.

Example 2.6

Dollars/Danish Kroner	6.6500–6.6550
Dollars/French francs	5.0000–5.0050

In other words, dollars can be sold in Paris and Copenhagen at the rates quoted in the left-hand column, and bought at the higher prices listed on the right.

A dealer wishes to sell Danish Kroner against French francs, but is forced to use the dollar quotations as the direct Danish Kroner/French francs rates in Paris and Copenhagen are not as competitive. To achieve this feat over the dollar quotations, he will first have to buy dollars against Danish Kroner at 6.655 and then he will have to sell the dollars in Paris for French francs at 5.0000. This means that the Danish Kroner/French francs rate would be obtained by dividing 5.000 by $6.655 \times 100 = 75.1314$. To ensure that the price in Paris equals the rate in Copenhagen, the standard reciprocal calculation of dividing 100 by $75.131 \times 100 = 133.100$ confirms the accuracy of the first rate.

It becomes evident from this example that when direct and indirect quotations are used to produce an unknown exchange rate, multiplication is the operative arithmetical exercise; whereas when two direct quotations are used, division produces the answer.

Naturally, whether computing reciprocal rates or straight quotations over two other rates, it is always advisable to prove the correctness of the calculations before quoting firm dealing prices. In a way it is better still if two individuals establish the rates using different approaches, *e.g.* one calculates French francs as quoted in Copenhagen, while the other finds the Danish

Kroner rate in Paris and they then apply the reciprocal method to prove the results. It is obviously unnecessary for a specialist in specific cross currency transactions to have his rates checked, as practice and theory will be second nature to him.

In Example 2.6, we departed from the sale of Danish Kroner against dollars, but it would not have made much difference if the dealer had first sold the dollars against French francs, before buying dollars against Danish Kroner. The only difference that could arise is that the result of a transaction over two currencies could leave a balance in the wrong currency. If the operator wished to buy an exact amount of French francs, for example, Ffr4,000,000, it would make good sense to buy the round amount of French francs first and then to proceed to buy the odd amount of dollars against Danish Kroner. Problems arise, however, when a dealer acting on behalf of a customer ends up with his profit (or loss) in a currency in which he has no active positions and the difference remains on the books, probably unnoticed for a long time.

There is a risk involved in trying to tie in two open-ended transactions, as the market may move before the bargain has been fully covered. The usual practice is to line up two banks in the appropriate centres, whether by telex or telephone, at the same time. As the foreign exchange market in major currencies also operates outside the respective countries of the currencies, there is, of course, no obligation or need to buy or sell French francs in Paris or Danish Kroner in Copenhagen. Very likely there are banks in other centres, *e.g.* London, Luxembourg, New York, willing to quote competitively for these currencies.

As cross conversions and reciprocal rates can lead to costly mistakes, aspirant dealers should spend time getting familiar with the principles and set themselves problems to solve.

Computers are rarely, if ever, programmed to cope with reciprocal rates. Input of primary or secondary transactions amounts may then have to be reversed to ensure that the right result is entered on the confirmation and more important, that the correct amount is paid or received.

Melded Rates

As it may be difficult to execute a large amount in one transaction, it is often necessary to spread the business among a number of contacts at better or worse rates than the original rate. To check that the overall rate obtained on the various transactions shows a profit or permits making a quotation to a customer who has placed a best order, the dealer will have to find the average rate. This is a tedious process but is essential to get the right melded rate.

Example 2.7

A trader has been instructed by a customer to buy 50 million US dollars against sterling. As the market is rather 'thin' the dealer contacts several friendly banks and eventually covers the whole amount by dealing in smaller sums on four occasions: *i.e.* US dollars 25 million, 15 million, 7.5 million and 2.5 million, and, of course, the rates on each deal differ. The dealer lists the transactions and simply multiplies the rates by 25, 15, 7.5 and 2.5 and then divides the total by 50 to obtain the average rate. (The figures in the far right-hand column below are obtained by dividing the dollar sums by their rate of exchange.)

Dollar sum	Rate of exchange	Total	
$25,000,000 at	2.2510 =	56.27500	£11,106,175.03
$15,000,000 at	2.2512 =	33.76800	£6,663,113.01
$7,500,000 at	2.2517 =	16.88775	£3,330,816.72
$2,500,000 at	2.2509 =	5.62725	£1,110,666.84
$50,000,000		112.55800	£22,210,771.60

$$\frac{112.558}{50} = 2.25116 \qquad \frac{\$50,000,000.00}{22,210,771.60} = 2.25116$$

Most numerate people will find averaging a simple application of logic, although they may get a little confused at times. Complications set in when a customer wishes to buy Deutsche Marks against sterling and finds it necessary to cover the requirement through the dollar market. Naturally, it will be impossible to achieve the same arithmetical neatness in the averaging process. Some rounding up or down of the amounts will be necessary but the operative principle remains the same. If it is assumed that a customer wishes to buy the Deutsche Mark equivalent of 50 million dollars against sterling, but will pay in sterling, the previous example can be expanded upon to produce the exact Deutsche Mark/sterling rate.

Example 2.8

Using the 50 million dollars bought against sterling the dealer contacts specialists in dollar/Deutsche Marks and manages to sell the dollars for Deutsche Marks in three 'goes': 30 million, 15 million and 5 million as follows:

$30,000,000 at 2.0000 =	60.00000		DM60,000,000
$15,000,000 at 2.0010 =	30.01500		DM30,015,000
$5,000,000 at 2.0005 =	10.00250		DM10,002,500
$50,000,000	100.01750		DM100,017,500

$$\frac{100.01750}{50} = 2.00035 \qquad \frac{DM100,017,500}{DM50,000,000} = 2.00035$$

Once the melded rates for sterling/dollar and dollar/Deutsche Mark have been established, it is standard procedure to calculate the sterling/Deutsche Mark rate by the normal method of multiplying the two rates (multiplication is necessary because indirect and direct quotations are involved, *i.e.* the two rates value different currencies, one sterling, the other the US dollar). The melded rate in this instance for the whole transaction is $2.00035 \times 2.25116 =$ DM4.503108

A number of liberties were taken with Example 2.8. Very few customers would approach a bank to buy a Deutsche Mark equivalent of 50 million dollars against sterling. It just suited our purpose to produce a neat arithmetical package. The situation would have been more a case of 'I would like to buy 50 or 100 million Deutsche Marks against sterling', with the best rate available only through the two dollar markets. As 50 or 100 million Deutsche Marks do not neatly translate into dollars or sterling, it might then have been easier to cover the round amount of Deutsche Marks against US dollars first and then to undo the dollars against sterling. However much care the operator exercises with the last transaction, a chain such as this one will leave odd amounts. He then either includes the amount in its entirety in the calculation or makes small adjustments up or down to make the computation less cumbersome. Care must be taken to ensure that the adjustment is not large enough to influence the overall result produced in the melded rate.

General Comments

Knowledge of how to convert one exchange rate to check the accuracy of another one or simply to establish a third rate is one of the most important skills a dealer requires. Arbitrage operations in spot rates generate profits but normally they are contributory factors applied to improve the overall result of special transactions. As the profit margins are mostly of negligible proportions, absolute accuracy in calculating the optimum conversion rates is vital, otherwise seemingly 'sure-fire' profit generators turn into loss leaders.

3

OUTRIGHT FORWARD RATES

Definition

The forward rate for a currency is the price at which this currency can be bought (or sold) for delivery on a future date.

In essence, there is little difference between the spot rate and the forward rate for a currency. Once the exchange rate for a forward deal has been agreed between two parties, the confirmation and settlement procedures are identical with those for a spot transaction. With the one exception of the end of the month forward value date, the convention to fix forward dates also follows the spot value pattern.

In reality, the spot rate for a currency is just as much a forward rate, especially if market conditions permit dealings to take place for same day (cash) or next day settlement. There are a number of risks attached to forward dealing which make it essential to exercise greater care than for a spot transaction. For instance, the forward rate is not purely a reflection of the strength or weakness of a currency but also allows for interest rate differentials, thus forward rates at times move even more dramatically than spot rates. On the other hand, the advantages outweigh such drawbacks. The ability to cover risks in the forward markets makes it easier for treasurers and dealers to fix the value of future assets and liabilities.

Distinction should be made between outright forward rates and swap rates (see Chapter 4). Though technically the fixing of outright forward exchange rates is based on the 'swap' rates for the appropriate periods, the exposure element of an outright forward operation is greater than that of a swap transaction.

Risks Attached to Forward Contracts

The longer the period of the forward contract the greater also the risk that the creditworthiness of the counterparty could deteriorate. It could happen that counterparties find themselves unable to meet the terms and conditions of a spot contract. This has happened in the past. Nevertheless, the danger of a spot transaction 'going sour' is smaller than a forward contract becoming null and void. The worst possible outcome of an exchange contract is that one of the contractants fulfils his side of the bargain, whereas the other party defaults. This could result in the loss of the principal amount or costly litigation. And, if the offending party could not meet the obligation at all, the exchange exposure might still have to be covered in the market at the going rate. Consequently, a further loss might be incurred when the open position has to be covered. However, the incidence of spot and forward contracts becoming null and void or resulting in one party losing the equivalent amount are negligible compared to the massive volume and infinite number of transactions consummated over the years.

As most of the trading volume is concentrated in the spot market, both the total volume and the number of participants decline the further forward the need for exchange cover is. With fewer competitors vying for business, the market-makers are in a position to dictate terms and to 'worsen' their prices by widening the margins between the buying and selling rates. In some cases, they may quote only the side of the market that suits them best in the light of their own positions or views of future trends.

For the market-maker the risk of being left with a forward 'gap' position is also greater. After satisfying the needs of his customer(s), he may find that there are no suitable counter offers or parties in the market to unwind the exposure, because the price is not right, or the amount is too large or too small, or worse still, because his name is not acceptable to the other side. And, of course, there is the possibility that the market-maker does not have an internal guidance line for the party with a counter interest. It may also happen that no offers or bids are available at all, in which case cover may have to be taken for a totally different value date, in the process creating a gap exposure. Although gap exposures are part and parcel of forward dealing, dealers prefer to initiate their own forward gap positions rather than being forced into them.

Advantages of Forward Contracts

On the plus side of covering operations in the forward market is the consideration that there is more room for manoeuvre, especially if the forward transaction is not against a specific asset or liability. Whereas a spot transaction has to be undone or carried forward almost immediately, a forward outright contract can be monitored and adjusted with time in hand.

The forward market is also of importance to company treasurers, as they can fix the cost of imports or exports in terms of the national unit of account well in advance of the time that payments have to be made or receivables converted. As long as the treasurer contracts with a reputable bank his only worry is that if for some reason the goods are not received or paid for, he will be left with an exposed currency position.

In spite of all the precautions taken, business ventures can go wrong and the fact that the foreign exchange cover is not required, and adds to the loss must be weighed against the many other occasions that timely cover has protected the profit margin on an import or export.

Professional dealers are in a much more flexible position than their commercial counterparts. Treasurers in commercial companies with limited access to market intelligence benefit even more if they cover in forward, thus avoiding use of the spot market when there is no more time for posturing. The rate, whether good or bad, must be accepted, as cover has to be generated 'willy-nilly'.

Normal and End of Month Forward Rates

For most major currencies, the market-maker and the user will have little difficulty in obtaining buying and selling prices for the standard maturities. Standard maturities are normally one, two, three, six, nine and twelve months, with longer and intermediate periods very much subject to negotiation. In the developed major currencies markets firm rates for four, five, seven, eight, ten and eleven months may also be quoted. However, maturities which do not conform to the standardized pattern are usually only serviced by a limited number of specialists. The more participants, high volume and numerous transactions there are, the more competitive and keen pricing will be. The influence of monetary policy and the lack of participants in the home country of the currency sometimes result in forward markets being restricted to maximum periods of six months.

The outright rates for forward currencies are based on the premiums and discounts of the swap market. It is usually assumed that premiums are deducted from the spot rate and conversely, that discounts are added to the spot rate. Of course, it must be borne in mind that only the currency priced is at a discount or premium, but more of that later. Forward rates are not quoted as outright prices, and most of the time there is no outright forward market. While commercial users of the foreign exchange market will be quoted outright forward rates, professionals know that their counterparts are only prepared to quote spot rates and forward margins.

Forward margins in a stable market reflect the effective interest rates in the countries of the two currencies involved in a forward transaction, or that used to be the case. Unless a country has no exchange controls at all, and no other official constraints, the effective interest rates are those applied in the free international market, the so-called Asian, Euro-or off-shore markets. Why and how the margins are calculated will be explained in detail in Chapter 5, Interest Arbitrage Operations. For outright dealing or covering it is sufficient to know that the forward rate is the spot rate plus or minus the forward margin, also referred to as premiums or discounts.

Premiums and discounts can cause confusion in the minds of the most expert traders, because they are a question of whose discounts and whose premiums. A London banker buying dollars for forward delivery at a rate lower than the spot rate will rationalize that the dollars are at a premium, *i.e.* more sterling has to be dispensed to buy forward dollars than to buy dollars for spot delivery. Conversely, the New York trader in the process of buying or selling sterling will consider sterling to be at a discount or premium. Hence the care that must be exercised when discussing premiums and discounts with contacts abroad. Slightly reiterative it may be, but it must be pointed out that current practice in the market, whether in New York or in London, is to deal sterling rather than dollars, in spite of the fact that commercial interests in the United Kingdom still think of dollars. These changes in the professional market are not usually noticed by outside users, but are important when obtaining the opinions of a bank dealer.

One convention that is generally accepted is that when the forward margins for buying or selling start with the higher number, the margins have to be deducted from the spot rates to establish the outright forward rates.

Example 3.1

Spot dollar/Deutsche Marks	2.0000–2.0005
One month margins	100– 95
One month outright rates	1.9900–1.9910

Whereas one dollar can be sold for DM2.0000 on the spot, only DM1.9900 will be received for one dollar delivered in one month's time.

Just as for spot transactions, there is a tendency to quote indirect rates in New York for forward deals against the national currency in the international market, as has been the case for sterling in London since the beginning of the market. More and more, dollars and sterling are the currencies which are traded in round amounts between professionals. Naturally, outsiders can always request to be quoted prices for round amounts of Deutsche Marks, Swiss francs or whatever, but in the interbank brokers' market, round amounts of dollars or sterling will be more acceptable. The 24-hour worldwide market which is developing necessitates this standardization of practices and amounts.

The calculations to convert one currency into another are also the same for spot and forward operations, once a rate acceptable to both parties has been agreed.

Odd Maturities

Maturities that fall outside the standard forward value date structure at the time of quoting can pose problems for market-maker and client alike, especially when there is no price available in the open market. A party interested in buying two and a half months' Deutsche Marks will find a seller most of the time, but may have to pay a little extra for the privilege and when selling will receive a little less than he would normally have done when acquiring or disposing of a currency for a standard forward date.

Example 3.2

Date	Period	Buying rate	Selling rate
1st	Spot	2.0000	2.0005
1st	1 month	100*	95
1st	2 months	200	195
1st	3 months	300	295

*This is instead of quoting 0.0100 which the market shortens to 100.

For the purpose of this example, the assumption is made that the months are of an equal duration of 30 days and that the buying and selling margins show a neat arithmetical progression which is rare in the real world. In practice, it is unusual for forward margins to show the same spread for each month, as the anticipation of currency movements and changes in the interest rate structure will result in different dealing attitudes being taken by market-makers and users for future delivery. Furthermore, the influence of technical periods in the money markets such as the end of the year will have an impact on the forward margins.

An interested party contacting a bank and expressing a wish to buy two and a half months' outright dollars could, at least in theory, expect to be quoted 2.0005 – 245 = 1.9760, maturing on the 16th of the third month. In the professional market it is, however, customary to ask for a two-way quote which leaves the market-maker in a quandary as to what side his customer is particularly interested in. As two and a half months is not a standard period, he would, then widen his quotation and instead of 250 – 245, he might quote 252 – 243, or, if he had already taken an exposure for that maturity date, or close thereto, he might quote one margin within the market range to ensure that if any dealing took place it would result in this position being cut, reversed or cancelled out. Then he might quote 254 – 249 or 249 – 244, or whichever way he feels that the customer may be attracted to do business but in a way that helps the market-maker out of a possible 'problem' situation.

Quite different considerations would come into the picture if a change in the interest rate structure of the US dollar and Deutsche Mark, or both, were anticipated sooner or later. Then the market-maker would have to take the view that, although the standard periods could be undone almost instantaneously, it would be quite a different matter if he were left with a gap exposure on his books as a result of dealing in this 'odd' period, because to cover an outright sale of two and a half months, he might have to buy in two months' or three months' dollars. Alternatively, he could straddle the date by buying half of the amount needed for two months' delivery and the remainder of the three months, thus taking a two-way bet. If he lost on one leg of the transaction, he would make good on the other one. In a way, if he felt reasonably sure about the way interest rates were going to move, he could even use the exposure created by his customer's needs to open a forward gap which, if the worst happened, would not cost him a fortune, but if the scenario he envisages materialized would produce a larger profit.

Odd Maturities (2)

Most dealers can cope with anticipated events by adjusting the forward price in such a way that an exposed maturity will not be vulnerable to devaluations or revaluations or their modern equivalent, depreciations or appreciations. To apply this knowledge is a routine affair. What is a more difficult task is to find a price for an odd maturity falling due close to a technical date: an end of the month, quarter, or year, taxation period, government funding times, etc. Then the dealer has to have in-depth knowledge of how these past events affected the interest and exchange rate structure of a currency.

That is why dealers will hesitate to quote odd maturities when they cannot with reasonable certainty quantify the effects of an anticipated event. And if they do quote, they will put in an insurance premium, which can make the price for an odd maturity too costly for the interested party. Technical periods which are known to the market will normally be 'flagged' by an illogical forward or interest rate dispersion for the near forward dates. For instance, historically the Swiss franc has been known to be in short supply at most year ends and often the market will prepare for this occurrence well in advance. The dealer knows that something is amiss simply by looking at the forward margins.

Example 3.3

On 15 November spot and forward US dollars against Swiss francs are quoted as follows:

Spot	1.9000–	1.9010
One month	150–	145
Two months	150–	145

Even the most inexperienced dealer would notice immediately that there is an inconsistency between the one and two month quotations, especially if the three months were priced at 200–195. A quick glance at his calendar will reveal the startling discovery that the one to two months' maturity straddles the end of the year. A problem would then only arise if a customer indicated an interest in buying or selling dollars for a date falling in the following year, particularly if the maturity occurred very early in January. Obviously, the forward margins indicate extreme tightness in the Swiss money market at the end of the year. Very likely this tightness will be more pronounced from the end of December until very early January because that is the period that extraneous factors such as 'window dressing', liquidity ratios, balance sheets, etc. are going to make their influence most felt.

Thus, the operator can conclude with a high degree of certainty, that once the end of the year is over and forgotten, the Swiss money market will revert to its low interest rates structure (compared with the yields on US dollars) and that consequently, the forward margins will again show the US dollar to be at a discount against Swiss francs in the forwards. Logically, the dealer can then reach the decision that he would prefer to sell Swiss francs for delivery in early January, or more correctly, to buy US dollars. Although, in this example, it is still the US dollar that is being bought and sold, the forward rates are primarily affected by the Swiss franc and for that reason the dealer could feel justified in thinking more in terms of buying and selling Swiss francs.

As the dealer has decided that he would rather buy than sell US dollars, the problem still remains of how to cover the exposure if his customer expresses the wish to buy dollars for delivery on 3 or 4 January. Selling dollars for delivery on 3 January would mean buying Swiss francs for that day. How to cover the risk would present a dilemma. To sell Swiss francs (buy dollars) for the one month maturity would mean having to borrow or swap Swiss francs over the tightest period, while, on the other hand, to sell Swiss francs for the two months approximately in the middle of January would mean having to dispose of them in early January when the Swiss money rates are expected to ease. Quite a predicament to be in. It would seem that this time the dealer may have to take the view that discretion is the better part of valour and quote his customer in such a way that the customer either refuses to deal or, if he deals on the rates, the dealer can enter the market and cover the exposure in the two months, leaving enough margin to absorb the cost he will have to incur in January when he has to undo the gap position.

As can be seen from the various examples, market-makers may quote outright prices but unless the transactions can be covered for the exact day, forward gap positions will have to be created.

In the example the operator was mainly worried about the effect the Swiss money market would have on the forward rates. However, the influence of the US dollar should not be ignored altogether. If a tightness of the Swiss market were accompanied by an easing in the US dollar money market, the dealer who had bought Swiss francs for delivery in early January and had covered the exposure by selling Swiss francs for December delivery would see his problem compounded by the exaggerated divergence in the interest rate structures, both *contra* to his position. If it were the other way around, he would have no worries, as a sale for delivery of francs in January, compensated by a purchase in December, would produce extra profits if the described scenario occurred. Unfortunately, if every favourable or un-favourable probability were taken into account when a speculative price has to be made, contradictory factors would inhibit dealers to such an extent that they might 'shut up shop' rather than take a risk.

Possible Exposures

Though foreign exchange dealers do make money by taking long or short positions in currencies, they cannot increase their exposures exponentially. In theory, though rarely in practice, it must be taken for granted that dealers cover every exposure they incur. This is in spite of the fact that the dates may differ. Taking everything into account, gap exposures are still less worrisome than outright exchange positions.

The reason for considering that all outright forward exchange risks must be covered immediately is that unless the market shows stability, with two-way dealing taking place most of the time, it is possible that the thrust may become one-way, *i.e.* more buyers than sellers, which eventually will result in a rate adjustment. And, if the market-maker kept meeting the market's needs (granted, at less and less competitive rates), it would still mean accumulating unacceptable exposures, which would be contrary to sound banking practices.

To put this particular example in a realistic context, based on the rather optimistic view that the customer is interested in buying Swiss francs for January delivery, it would be logical to calculate that Swiss francs will return to the easiness displayed before the end of the year once normal dealing resumes in January. Thus from 2 January to the 17th, the proportionate forward rate must be roughly half of the one month margin, *i.e.* $145 \times 0.5 = 72.5$. As a slight protection will be incorporated in the quote, the half month may be adjusted to 70 or whatever margin the dealer considers appropriate for taking the risk. As the two months' outright rate for selling Swiss francs (buying dollars) is $1.9000 - 150 = 1.8850$ the customer may be quoted $1.8850 + 70(?) = 1.8920$.

Why use was made of the 145 rather than the 150 side is simply that dealers should always take the view that the worst will happen and that they will be forced to cover their exposures at the worst rate available in the market. And to cover the gap from 2 January until the 17th would necessitate the sale of dollars (purchase of Swiss francs) on the 2nd and the simultaneous purchase of dollars (sale of Swiss francs) for value on 17 January. For this operation the market is anticipated to show half of the current one month spread based on 145 – the least advantageous side. It could even be argued that a 70 point adjustment is too generous and that 50 or lower still would be a more realistic price for taking on an exposure which can only be undone once dealing starts for January spot dates.

The covering position will have to be effected for value on 17 January, as this is a less exposed gap position, rather than taking out cover for value on 17 December. However, what would happen if the operator in a mood of bravado decided to buy Swiss francs for 17 December (selling dollars) because he felt that Swiss interest rates would have to tighten further or dollar rates ease? Although the one month dollar/Swiss franc is quoted, this rate would not provide a viable basis for computing the price for delivery on 2 January. A quotation for value on 2 January would still have to be backtracked to the price made for 17 January. The dealer would be taking more of a gamble and the rate of 1.8920 might have to be lowered further as a change in the abnormal pattern could easily occur, leaving the dealer with a loss situation.

Of course, by quoting uncompetitive rates the dealer might lose not only the business but also the opportunity of bidding for future business from that particular customer. If the customer desperately required cover he might contact another dealer either with a position permitting the transaction to take place at a better rate, or one more inclined to take a gamble on a favourable outcome.

Cross Currency Forward Rates

The figuring out of forward cross currency rates (outright) follows broadly the same rationale as that for spot rates. Complications set in when it is necessary to go through the dollar/Deutsche Mark spot and forward rates and the sterling/dollar forward rates to establish an outright forward sterling/Deutsche Mark price or similar conversion processes with other currencies. The principles that should always be applied are that the market-maker should use whichever rates are the most beneficial to him, and that the customer must take into account that a quotation he obtains will nearly always reflect the most expensive side of the market for the type of transaction he has in mind. (*See* spot cross rate conversions, pages 11 and 12).

Naturally, odd maturities and non-standard forward dates will accentuate the problem and add to the likelihood that the quoter may make a mistake in his calculations. That could be to the advantage of the customer, but not necessarily so. Again, it must be stated that the user should point out major quotation errors, although he is quite justified in assuming that minor divergences from the norm reflect the market-maker's view of what the exchange rates should be.

Forward Options

A buyer of a forward option, or for that matter a seller, will be dealing on an outright basis. There are different kinds of options. A mutual option would be a waste of time and this practice has long since been dropped from the range of foreign exchange products. Only buyer's and seller's options remain in operation and even then these options are not normally available to the professional trader or the experienced treasurer in a large multinational or national corporation.

The reason for this lack of trust among professionals is simply that a professional who did not take advantage of a favourable development and realized his option would not be doing his job properly. It is slightly different for a genuine commercial interest, as the latter would be assumed to have a commercial transaction to back up the option contract. For example, options are of particular benefit to a commercial party not in a position to determine the exact arrival or departure dates of imports or exports.

Determining the Length of an Option Period

Option contracts can be for distant maturities although most times the actual option period will be limited to the shortest possible time span. In some export transactions covering capital goods, these option lengths can be for as long as six months.

With some hesitation, it could be said that the shorter the option period the better it is for the buyer or seller of the option. In most cases this statement holds true, as the option period is the time the option writer is most exposed. In most instances he is a market-maker, but this is not always true because many banks not regularly involved in market-making will be quite prepared to offer option facilities to genuine customers and then to cover the pure exchange risk for a fixed maturity in the professional market.

How is an option period decided upon? An importer may have negotiated a contract to import a machine tool from abroad and whether the transaction is covered by a documentary credit or on an open account basis, it is likely that between the time of negotiation and the actual arrival of the machine tool three to six months will have elapsed. If the exporter is of a generous disposition there may also be a credit facility built into the contract. Thus, it could be that the machine tool could arrive any time between the three and six months and that payment would be due in six to nine months. It is assumed, of course, that the exporter is invoicing in his own, or in another foreign currency, otherwise there would be no need to worry about exchange cover.

The importer is naturally interested in making sure that the cost of the machine tool will not be higher than the amount he contracted for, but his problem is the uncertainty about the date of payment. If he has done business in the past with the same party abroad under roughly the same conditions, he may have some idea of how long it will take for the machine to arrive and payment to be due. Given the earliest the shipment can be expected is in four months' time (but is unlikely to exceed five) and barring acts of God or strikes, he can be reasonably certain that sometime between the seven and eight months payment will have to be made and either now or at a later date the foreign currency will have to be acquired. Knowing the approximate timing he can then contact his bank and explain that he would like to be quoted for a buyer's option to run from the seven to eight months' forward date. It is always preferable to buy or sell options periods in dealing months, as prices for these standard periods are usually available up to one year in the major currencies.

The bank writing the option can take the view that it is better to cover the exposure by buying or selling early during the option period, or they may decide to buy or sell for the last date or middle of the period, based on previous experience they have had with the buyer of the option. The beneficiary of an option who has proved in the past that he does not make a habit of taking advantage of favourable developments once the option is callable, may expect preferential treatment. Preferential treatment would mean an improvement in the absolute terms the bank would quote for the option. Instead of applying the worst rate, the market-maker might shade the rate a mite, giving the customer a better deal in the process, in the hope that he will use the bank again for future transactions. Repeat business is what a bank looks for when quoting competitively.

As for all exchange quotations, the option rates are based on the worst possible outcome for the quoting bank and consequently the worst rate for the client.

Applying the option procedure to a hypothetical import transaction into the United Kingdom, the customer and the bank would act in the following manner:

Example 3.4

UK Limited has been informed by its American suppliers that goods contracted for will be delivered in five months' time. The invoice is to be denominated in US dollars and the payment due as soon as the goods reach the appropriate UK port.

UK Limited knows from experience that the American suppliers run a fairly efficient organization and if they say that the consignment will arrive in about five months this should be the case.

Naturally, delays in the US, the weather, etc., can delay the arrival of the shipment by a matter of a few weeks. This means that ideally

UK Limited should ensure availability of US dollars some time between the five and six months.

In the past the UK company may have purchased dollars for fixed forward maturities, but has found that this practice creates problems when the contract has to be prematured or extended, as it is well-nigh impossible to arrange cover for the exact day payment is due. Possibly UK Limited may have incurred losses as a result of covering the wrong date or has had the added worry of monitoring the maturities of the fixed-term contracts to ensure that they are adjusted for the appropriate value date when this is known. This time the company has made the conscious decision to ensure availability without other complications and has considered the purchase of a US dollar option for the optimum period between the five and six months.

UK Limited contacts a bank in the City of London and indicates an interest in buying dollars for the five to six months' option period. It is, of course, necessary to disclose a buying or selling interest for an option, as the bank will be disinclined to quote option prices without knowing which way the customer's interests lie.

The bank in the City will then either use its own quotations or check the rates in the market which have a bearing on the option price. The rates the bank obtains are:

Spot	2.2510– 15
Five months	225–215
Six months	265–255

In the first place the bank will have to look at the worst possible outcome that could develop. The customer can exercise his option at any time between the five and six months. He might not take up the option until the last day (corresponding with the six months' date), which would appear, at least at the outset, the most inauspicious value date for the bank. Consequently, the dealer will have to compute his rate on the six months' quotation and will price the option at not worse than 2.2510 – 265 = 2.2245. The dealer would have had to base his initial price on the view that, as the customer does not have to take up his option until the six months' date, this particular option is identical to a normal outright sale for six months' delivery.

Given the rates shown in the schedule hold good for another client interested in selling dollars for the same option period, then obviously the bank would use the buying spot rate of 2.2515 – 215 = 2.2300. The dealer would not give the benefit of the six months' rate to the customer, as the latter might exercise the option on the first day, *i.e.* the date corresponding with the standard five months' maturity date. The reasoning of the dealer is the reverse of that applied to the buyer's option contract. He hopes that his customer will refrain from exercising the option until the last day open to him. In other words, both for buying and selling options – assuming there is no change in the forward rate structure – the first and the last day respectively would seem the optimum days in so far as the foreign currency (US dollars) is at a premium.

Covering an Option

There are conflicting opinions on how an option should be covered. The purist view is that an option should be covered for the first day the option can be exercised, that is:

> – when granting a buyer's option obtain cover for the first option day;
> – when granting a seller's option, sell for the first option day.

In principle everything is fine if the beneficiary of an option does exactly that. But in practice that would be too much to expect. The more adventurous approach is to match the exposure by buying or selling for the last option date. This approach assumes that whatever happens a customer will not call his option until the last day and that the market-maker is in a position to forecast the short-date forward structure at some time in the future. Both extremes carry risks and are contrary to the philosophy that all dealing risks should be brought back to an acceptable level. As with most things in life, the middle way would seem the most prudent one. If at all possible, a five to six months' option whether buying or selling, should be covered somewhere in the middle (*see* option contract cover schedule, page 31). For relatively short options of up to six months, the dealer usually has a fairly good idea of what the forward rates should be towards the maturity of the deal. Or, at least, he knows whether they will be at a premium or discount.

Whether an option transaction will produce a profit or loss is usually decided by the short-term rates at the time the option is exercised. This potential loss situation can be minimized by taking out cover for a date which will be closest to the day the option will be exercised. The narrowing or widening of premiums or discounts in changing markets can have a detrimental effect. Longer options are more vulnerable in every respect, longer in maturity, that is, as well as in the actual option time.

Once a dealer has fixed the rate which is in his judgement the worst based on current market prices, he can start to tinker with the competitiveness of the quotation. Or, he may decide to worsen the rate as the future exchange rate and, *ipso facto*, the interest rate structure seem uncertain. He must also include past experience with the beneficiary of the option in his deliberations. How has the customer handled previous options or ordinary exchange transactions?

A specialist in options with numerous contacts and buyers and sellers of options in the same currencies can afford to be more adventurous than one with only one (or a few) large customers with long-term options.

Short-term Options

It might be interesting to look at the dealer's approach when the US dollar is at a discount against sterling, as in the following schedule.

Example 3.5

Spot rate	2.2510–2.2515	
Five months	215–	225
Six months	255–	265

(Although on several occasions over the last 25 years US dollars have been at a discount against sterling in the forward market, most of the time dollars have been at a premium, as sterling interest rates were higher as a consequence of sterling being under pressure in the exchange markets. Times change and the relative strength of sterling over the last few years has resulted in a fundamental change in that sterling has at times commanded a premium over the dollar in the forward market. This change in emphasis is also a reflection of lower interest rates in the UK.

If the buyer of a five against a six months' option now went to his banker, he would get a different story. Instead of being charged the six months' rate, the professional dealer would apply the five months' rate, thus: 2.2510 + 215 = 2.2725. The buyer definitely would not get the benefit of the longer maturity. Because the dollar is at a discount, it is no longer of advantage to the dealer to have the buyer exercise his option on the first day, on the contrary, the last day is now the optimum delivery day for the option writer. If the buyer took up his option on the first day the market-maker would have to enter the market to buy dollars for the option date against any forward date he had originally chosen to cover the exposure.

When a currency is at a premium in the forwards and is expected to remain so, it is advisable to take the cover in no earlier than the middle date of the option period for a buyer's option. The worst that can happen then is that the buyer takes delivery on the last possible day. And, subject to previous experience, the countervalue of a seller's option should be sold for delivery not later than the middle of the option period.

The magnitude of anticipated forward levels has, of course, a bearing on the decision whether to cover early or late during the option period. In many active dealing banks it is not even standard practice to cover option contracts unless they are for substantial amounts or for very long maturities.

When a forward currency is at a discount and educated guesses indicate that this will be the case when the option period arrives, it is usually safer to cover a buyer's option for the first maturity date and the seller's option as far into the period as possible. The worst that could happen is that the buyer of an option takes delivery on the first day, and a seller postpones exercising his right until the very last day.

It would be unwise to look at option quotations as direct or indirect rates. It is preferable to consider the currency used as the basis for the price as the home currency, and the currency that is being priced as the foreign one. For instance, when dollars/Deutsche Marks are quoted in Deutsche Mark terms, then it is obviously the US dollar which is at a premium or discount in the forward market. Even when a customer desires to buy Deutsche Marks against dollars it would be more logical to think of this transaction as a purchase of dollars. Then the normal process of 'how do we buy or sell dollars?' can be applied.

Probably the sterling/dollar option contract examples (*see* pages 26 and 29) should have been couched in terms of buying or selling sterling, rather than buying or selling dollars. However, option contracts are usually entered into with commercial counterparts and in the United Kingdom these commercial interests very likely would look at the dollar as the foreign currency, which makes it more difficult to switch from thinking in dollar to sterling terms. The same consideration would not apply in the United States where sterling would definitely be the foreign currency. (While an indirect quotation example was used for the first option example, the rationale for direct quotations would be the same.)

A commercial customer contacting a bank in Frankfurt with an interest in buying dollars for delivery at his option between the two and three month period would set in motion the normal information gathering process. The West German market-maker would first find out the rates in the standard periods.

Example 3.6

Spot dollar/Deutsche Marks	2.0000– 05
One month	100– 95
Two months	200–195
Three months	300–295

As for odd maturities, whether in sterling/dollars or any other currency, the bank dealer would naturally check whether the two to three months straddled a technical situation which could have beneficial or detrimental results if the client exercised his option at an inopportune time. This factor would have to be built into the price. However, in this instance there are no technical features which could have an impact on the transaction. Then, with the customer interested in buying dollars, the rate would be based on the spot selling rate for dollars (2.0005, less the margin for the two months, 195), arriving at a price of 1.9810. As for the sterling/dollars example (*see* Example 3.4, page 26), any favourable adjustment would have to be based on previous experience.

The best possible outcome for the bank would be that the customer refrained from calling the dollars until the very last day but this would be too much to expect. The improvement in the rate would depend very much on whether the odds were in favour of the customer not exercising his option until late in the period, which might encourage the bank to make a gesture, such as a favourable adjustment in the option rates, in the hope that the customer will show his appreciation by continuing to transact business with the bank.

An early realization of this buyer option would leave the bank short of dollars (although long of Deutsche Marks) and to roll this exposure forward to the cover date would mean giving up part of the profit or even turning the transaction into a loss. The bank would only gain more if the dollars changed from a discount to a premium in the forward market and with the forward structure as indicated this appears highly unlikely.

Although an ultra-conservative attitude would encourage covering the exposure by buying dollars for the first option date (two months), the probability of the option being called on the first day is negligible and cover taken out for the middle of the period would limit the risk of the position having to be unwound for a whole month.

The posturing of the market-makers to limit an option exposure risk can be summarized as follows:

Option contract cover schedule			
	Rate for buyer's option	*Rate for seller's option*	*Cover date*
Forward premium	Last day		Middle of period or later
Forward premium		First day	Middle of period or earlier
Forward discount	First day		Middle of period or earlier
Forward discount		Last day	Middle of period or later

Basic assumptions should include the view that there will be little change in the forward structure, and, concomitantly, the relationship of the interest rates for the two currencies will remain at the existing equilibrium. All the same, the giver of the option will try to protect himself from what he considers the worst possible outcome.

To overcome the problem of deciding which currencies are at a premium or discount in the above schedule we must assume that the currency which is being priced in terms of another one is being sold or bought.

Long-term Options

For long-term options, six months or longer, especially when the amounts involved are substantial, it would be safer still to take out cover spread over the period of the option. A wholesale covering operation for one maturity date would leave the option writer too exposed to the vagaries of the market. Furthermore, large option contracts and their cover should be monitored all the time and the maturity date structure adjusted to reflect money market events or trends. Of course, when the cover is spread over the whole period there is less need to take evasive action when no definite future pattern has been established.

General Comments

Option dealing, while providing greater security to the beneficiary, can also be a profitable venture for the dealer if the positions are created with some forethought. Unfortunately, as was stated at the beginning of the option section, the liberalization of the markets makes it far more difficult for the professional dealers to gain extra profits on options, as large national and multinational companies are staffed by traders who know the markets just as well as their counterparts in the banks.

Ante-spot Value Dates

For lack of a better description, value dates pre-dating spot – same day (cash) and next day – can be looked at as ante-forward dates. The spot date is a forward date and for reporting purposes many monetary authorities consider only balances carried on the reporting day in nostro accounts as spot positions. Open transactions carried for value next day and spot are considered to form part of the forward book of an organization. This approach is logical, as in a developed currency market positions created for the next day and even the same day can be unwound or carried forward to another maturity.

At one time dealing was possible for the same day in most of the major currencies. However, to discourage speculation and to put obstacles in the way of those wishing to make quick profits, many central banks have instituted clearing procedures which make it imperative that instructions reach the paying or receiving banks the previous day or not later than very early on the settlement day. Also, value same day dealing is really only practicable when the currency to be settled is that of a country in a later time zone, such as US and Canadian dollars when dealing from Europe. The US dollar can be traded in London until late in the afternoon on a deposit basis for same day delivery, although for foreign exchange against sterling the banks are limited by the fact that the sterling clearing closes at 3.00 p.m. With a five- or six-hour favourable time difference, there is ample time to telex or telephone instructions to the New York correspondents.

Time constraints on dealing in the near maturity dates make it difficult to speculate for these deliveries. The market has, however, adjusted to this fact and these days banks tend to take open short or long positions for future delivery, making it more difficult for other participants to know what they are doing and giving themselves more time to wait for favourable developments without having to worry about covering the immediate shortage or disposing of a surplus. As short-date maturities tend to over-emphasize liquid or illiquid conditions, the proportionate cost of these maturities is usually far greater than for the longer maturities, which is another encouragement for the speculator to take the forward route.

The fact that the base date for exchange transactions falls on the spot date can result in a mental blockage for dealers who are used to dealing for outright spot or spot against forward dates, or even one forward date against another. Dealings for value same or next day are normally handled as swap transactions in the same way that one, two, three months, etc. are treated. The dealer buys or sells the currency for the same or next day and does the reverse operation for the following day or spot. Same value day until the next day and the next day to spot are quoted in margin terms just like ordinary forwards margins for standard maturities. Confusion, however, sometimes reigns when a customer or correspondent wishes to buy or sell outright for value same or next day. (Value next day is the first 'good' day after the transaction day. Obviously, when the transaction day falls on a Friday, the next 'good' day is the following Monday for most currencies.)

Short-date swaps are quoted (like normal forward rates) as premiums or discounts: *e.g.*

Today/tomorrow	2–1 or 3–4
Tomorrow/next	2–1 or 1–2

When a customer then expresses an interest in buying or selling for one of these ante-spot days the straightforward approach for fixing the forward outright rates has to be adjusted. In straight outright forward dealing no difficulty is encountered when putting together the worst price for a customer, usually it is a simple matter of deducting or adding the margin for the appropriate period. To apply a logical approach to a shorter than spot outright transaction is a little more complex.

Example 3.7

Spot dollar/Deutsche Mark	2.0000–05
Tomorrow/spot	2– 1
Today/tomorrow	2– 1

If these were normal forward rates, to construct an outright rate it would be sufficient to deduct 2 and 2 from the buying rate for spot and come up with 1.9996 for value same day outright. Conversely, the selling rate for same day value would become 2.0003. But that would be wrong. To establish ante-spot outright rates the quotations have to be reversed.

Based on the above rates, the market-maker, who has to quote a price at which he would sell dollars for value same day, would have to go through the following thinking process: 'Spot is 2.0005, but if I sell dollars for the same day, I shall have to enter the market to buy dollars for same day delivery and sell them for spot.' Why he has to think like that is simply because there is no established outright market for same or next day outright currencies, even in dollars. And even if he found another market-maker willing to deal outright for these ante-spot dates, the counterparty would have to take the short-date swap considerations into account before quoting and the user would have to be capable of checking the accuracy of the quotes. In any case, the first or second market-maker would have to buy dollars for same day value and sell them for spot, for which date, assuming he is of a conservative disposition, cover will have been effected.

In the process he would have 'given away' two points for each day, or four points in all and to get compensated for this cost, he would have had to add the four points to the spot price just to break even, or in other words, he would have had to quote 2.0009 to sell dollars for value same day delivery.

Consequently, the principle for fixing ante-forward rates is the reverse of the one applied to forward outrights. The order of the margins has to be reversed and more important, whereas a forward discount is deducted from the spot rate, the ante-spot margin, if a discount will have to be added to the quote, is as follows:

Example 3.8

Spot dollar/Deutsche Marks	2.0000–05	
Tomorrow/spot	1– 2	(instead of
Today/tomorrow	1– 2	2–1)

The normal discount/premium computations can then be followed, premium added and discount deducted from the outright spot prices. Accordingly, outright dollars against Deutsche Marks for next day value would be priced at 2.0001–2.0007 and for same day value 2.0002–2.0009.

Possible Exposures

Obviously, by quoting the exact rates for outright same or next day delivery, the market-maker would leave himself wide open to the volatile short-date markets. If a sale were executed for value same day, the operator would only have a few hours to unwind the exposure – given this was the only position he had on his books. He would either, before or after the event, have to acquire dollars for that value date, and that would entail buying dollars value same day and selling either next day or spot. Furthermore, he would have to purchase the dollars for spot delivery to cancel the exchange exposure. Naturally, a 'one off' transaction of this type would be costly to handle, as to undo the risk would necessitate at least three deals or more if the original amount traded were too large for another market-maker to absorb in one 'go'. The risk element is considerable as well, as there is no time for manoeuvre; the transaction is a loss or a profit and this is realized, which is different from a longer-term forward where the risk taker can lengthen or shorten the exposure and create more acceptable positions in the hope of eventually turning a potential loss situation into a profitable one.

Specialists in short-date transactions will make it their business to transact large volumes on both sides of the market. In this case they might well realize larger profit margins than spot or forward dealers, as the difference for two-way same day spot deals is wider than for most spot and forward transactions. This assumes, of course, that the market does not move against the operator, or if it does the adjustment is in his favour.

The market-maker would have to be reasonably certain that the market will remain stable, or he would have to anticipate that the spot rate and/or ante-forward rates will move in his favour, that is, if he decided to run either the outright risk or the swap risk for a very short period of time. Ante-spot margins, as mentioned previously (*see* page 33), can be extremely fickle as they respond to the immediate shortfalls and surpluses in the international and national money market for the currencies involved in a transaction. Consequently, the margins for ante-spot transactions are likely to reflect these temporary imbalances more dramatically than the standard forward maturities.

Using the Indirect System

When the ante-spot principle is applied to an indirect system, for instance, in the United Kingdom, the same approach will have to be adopted even though the operator may be buying and selling dollars rather than sterling.

Example 3.9

Spot sterling/dollar	2.2510–15
Tomorrow/next	2– 1
Today/tomorrow	1– 2

Whether looked at from New York or from London, one of these overnight margins is at a discount and the other at a premium. (A customer in the United Kingdom requesting a firm price for value same day against dollars would be treated in the same fashion as a customer in West Germany would.)

With the spot rate at 2.2510–15, the tomorrow/next day margin will be reversed to 1–2 (instead of 2–1) and the today/tomorrow margin would be turned round as well to 2–1 (instead of 1–2). It so happens that in this example it does not matter whether the rates are reversed or not as long as the price is for value same day.

However, it is still safer to go through the mechanics rather than to cut corners. Accordingly, to quote the customer his price the dealer would either mentally or on paper rationalize that:

If spot	2.2510–15		
Tomorrow/next		1– 2	(instead of 2–1)
Today/tomorrow		2– 1	(instead of 1–2)
Then outright	2.2509–16		

As most computers are programmed to deduct or add discounts and premiums and ante-margins reverse the normal trend, programmes in future will have to allow for this inconsistency when ante-spot outright rates have to be manufactured.

General Comments

In view of the number of transactions required to bring outright ante-spot transactions to a satisfactory conclusion, dealers tend to shy away from these situations. They prefer to operate on the spot markets where there is hardly any duplication of effort. As was pointed out earlier in the book, the spot market should be the haven of last resort for the commercial user of the exchange market. The outsider should avoid same and next day dealings like the plague. In extreme crisis conditions, the market goes haywire and then foreign exchange dealers are more concerned with their positions further in the future and will tend to quote very uncompetitive rates, as they are aware that to undo outright ante-dates is a complicated business. To be recompensed for the time and the risk the margins will then widen and even become unrealistic in comparison with the underlying ante-swap rates. Whereas the large multinational and national companies usually have sufficient influence to force their banking contacts to execute their orders, the same cannot be said for the smaller users who may not make the same impact.

One of the reasons that the interests of professional traders and commercial customers are diametrically opposed is simply the fact that the dealings in the interbank market are based on margins, while the users are mainly concerned with outright exchange exposures. One would hope that enterprising banks will quote ante-spot and forward rates as a matter of course, particularly when making prices to non-professionals.

4

SWAP TRANSACTIONS

With tongue in cheek, it could be said that spot dealing in currencies is the preserve of the gambler and speculator, while forward dealing – particularly, constructive forward dealing on one's own account – is an activity which gives intellectual enjoyment to the foreign exchange purist. Forward dealing and position taking are, apart from being business ventures, more akin to games of skill. When interest arbitrage is superimposed on the normal swap dealing, the matter becomes even more intricate and complex. It is still a form of gambling, but is less a matter of tossing a coin or outwitting the opposition as is the case in spot dealing. Spot dealing is a question of tactical short-term decisions, whereas forward and interest arbitrage dealing involve strategy, the longer-term view. However, before elaborating on and eulogizing the superiority of forward and forward/forward dealing over spot, it might be more appropriate to define the subject of this chapter.

Definition

A swap transaction is the simultaneous buying and selling of a foreign currency in approximately equal amounts for different maturity (settlement) dates.

Advantages of Swap Transactions

The immediate point to make is that a swap operation eliminates most of the exchange exposure. This is in contrast to an outright transaction which is a pure foreign exchange risk. Although the currency is bought and sold simultaneously for different value dates, and in theory it could be said that each transaction is a separate operation, in practice the markets only operate on a swap basis for forward maturities. Thus while an exposure is incurred only between the maturity dates, this gap can be narrowed or completely undone without too much trouble in the developed currency markets. In other words, the exposure can be reversed. The currencies bought and sold for different maturity dates, can be sold and bought, in fact effecting a reverse swap.

If the currencies cannot be bought or sold, they can be borrowed or lent for the period of the swap. The latter operation, though bringing the original transaction to a satisfactory conclusion, in itself entails finding suitable borrowers or lenders. In the professional market these counterparties would usually be found in the banking or near-banking sectors, as it may be difficult to identify creditworthy commercial borrowers and lenders to mesh in the maturity structure of a swap. Commercial interests rarely have the flexibility to take or place funds for six months when really they are only interested in shorter or longer periods. Furthermore, the currencies of the swap transaction may not suit the commercial placer or taker of funds.

Possibly the definition of a swap should be amended to read: buying or selling of a foreign currency for a near date and effecting an opposing transaction for a future value date, but dotting the 'i's' in this way would be superfluous, as in all exchange transactions one currency is being sold and another bought and one of these currencies can be the national unit of account, though not necessarily so. There are certain advantages attached to a domestic bank operating only against its national currency, as especially short positions in the national currency can be covered at lower cost than if a foreign currency had to be obtained in a similar manner. And even the latter statement does not always hold true, as there are situations when open or hidden foreign exchange controls make it more expensive to use the national currency within the borders of a nation, than for a non-resident to obtain the funds outside the country.

Parity

It is extremely rare that the two legs of a swap transaction can be accomplished without a net difference showing up in one of the two currencies. When both the near and the far side of a swap transaction are equal in amount and consequently, the same exchange rate is applied, it must follow that the effective interest rates for the two currencies are at par, or around par. It is rare for this to happen but not altogether unknown. The parity is usually on one side of the quotation rather than in the middle, as similar interest rates may not necessarily lead to moneys flowing across frontiers, as little advantage is to be gained either way. The pricing policy of the market-makers will ensure that the only beneficiaries of such situations are the professionals, if there are any beneficiaries at all.

In some instances money can still flow in and out between countries with interest rates close to the parity simply because taxation or other considerations make it advantageous for citizens of one of the countries to place their funds on deposit in the other country.

The roughly equal amounts will be impossible to attain, especially when the interest rate structure for two currencies differs substantially. Naturally, the forward margins will reflect this differential. For instance, if the operative interest rates for some maturities in Swiss francs are 4 per cent per annum and similar periods in sterling are closer to 15 per cent per annum, then the swap differential will be approximately 11 per cent per annum. That would mean that a purchase of £1,000,000 on the spot would cost 11 per cent more than an outright purchase of £1,000,000 for delivery in one year, both, of course, against Swiss francs. It is clear that if £1,000,000 is bought on the spot and the same amount is sold for one year settlement, the Swiss francs equivalent in one year's time will be 11 per cent less than the spot countervalue, consequently both parties will be left with unequal amounts.

Swaps and Outright Forward Operations

In Chapter 3, Outright Forward Rates, some of the peculiarities of forward dealing have already been explained in detail, although emphasis was placed on how the margins affected outright forward exchange quotations rather than why forward margins exist at all.

In effect, outright forward exchange transactions are sometimes the origin of swap transactions, albeit involuntarily. The simultaneous buying and selling is the theoretical approach favoured by forward specialists, whereas in the real world swaps are occasionally created when a dealer finds that an outright transaction cannot be undone for the exact maturity date. He will try to obtain cover for the nearest possible value date, but this still results in a forward gap and the overall transaction becomes a swap. By turning the outright exchange exposure into a swap, assuming that he is correct in his view of what will happen to the forward margins, the dealer can then possibly turn an unrealized loss into an actual profit.

It would be exceptionally fortunate if a large outright loss could be turned into a profit in this way, as the forward margins are normally less volatile than spot prices. And to make good a large outright loss might mean taking a long-term gap exposure and 'lady luck' being on the side of the dealer who has taken the view. On the whole, this is not a satisfactory way to manage forward exposures, as the gaps opened up as a result of outright deals may be *contra* to the general market trend and might well be *contra* to the positions taken on the forward book previously.

An even less satisfactory way of covering outright risks in the forward market by creating forward gaps is the conversion of an outright spot loss transaction into a forward swap by buying or selling the countervalue for a forward date. But, as these days most banks separate the duties of spot and forward dealers, this is less likely to happen. The interests of the forward dealer are not the same as those of the spot expert. This practical organizational conflict of interests inhibits to some extent the creation of forward gaps to hide outright losses.

The classical swap is, of course, the interaction of dealers taking opposite views of how the forward margin trends between two currencies will interact, influenced by effective interest rates. It can also be one dealer unloading a position previously taken with another market participant. These views take into account how pressures in the exchange market will widen or narrow the spreads for different periods, as well as the behaviour of interest rates in the two local money markets, or for that matter the effective interest rates operational in the international market.

Like long-term swap transactions, very short-term swaps (today/tomorrow or tomorrow spot up to spot to one month) are either right or wrong, unless the difference of, let us say, the one month margin compared to the very short term is such that over the period profits can be generated. Whether in reality these operations are cost effective depends on the expenses incurred by having to process numerous transactions. The longer the period of the swap, the more room there is for manoeuvre and time to adjust its length and magnitude.

The main advantage of effecting swaps as a means of creating forward maturities is that the participants do not have to worry about outright exchange movements, as these do not have great impact on the forward structure unless a major exchange rate adjustment is in the offing. Marginal up and down movements of the exchange rate will not influence forward margins greatly.

Forward Dealing

Accidental or Involuntary Swap Transactions

In an active dealing room involuntary swaps are created all the time. This is not only because outright forward operations cannot be undone unless a loss is realized, but is also as a result of the relatively small deals customers and correspondent banks bring to the market-makers. Quite often these transactions are miniscule compared with the wholesale activities in the interbank market. With the exception of small amounts in the minor and exotic currencies, small orders cannot be executed in the interbank market, as they would be too expensive to process. The processing costs of a $10,000,000 deal are no greater than those for $10,000; in effect, a smaller transaction engaged in with a commercial client may cost more, as greater care will have to be exercised to ensure that the countervalue is paid to the right account or the right beneficiary.

To handle customers' orders in the most efficient way, banks have to accumulate sufficient volume for one particular settlement day and this may prove difficult, if not impossible. The only approach open to them is to cover the scattered maturities for the most appropriate mid-point and sometimes this can be achieved by simply using positions created either by other users or correspondent operations.

Using Forward Positions

How these forward positions arise can be best explained in the following example.

Example 4.1

1   Early in the morning a dealer buys from a customer
    on the spot.   FC1,000,000
2   Another party buys for delivery in one month's
    time.   (FC1,500,000)
3   Still later in the day a correspondent bank sells for
    delivery on the six months' date.   FC   500,000

                                    Balance   FC   NIL

(FC = Foreign Currency)

Most dealers would like to deal on this basis all the time. Unfortunately it almost never happens. Commercial trades are rarely covered dollar for dollar, or Deutsche Mark for Deutsche Mark without the dealer having to take some decisive action for himself. It would be pure Utopia if the dealer did not have to act. Furthermore, the amounts bought and sold by customers will not display the arithmetical neatness of the example. Many times items like 33,333.33, etc. will have to be absorbed in the positions, either direct or at some reporting stage when retail departments in the bank disclose their dealings in foreign currencies. To arrive at a balanced position at the end of the day, without having to enter the market, would be miraculous. Most days small or large balances will be left on the spot and forward dealing accounts. This can create difficulties, as it may be troublesome to identify and allocate these currency imbalances to the forward or the spot dealer.

The net result of the rather elementary transactions itemized in Example 4.1 is two open forward positions:

a   the dealer is long FC1,000,000 on the spot against the one month, and
b   short of FC500,000 one month against six months.

A relatively minor gap exposure for a bank so long as the foreign currency units do not represent an inordinate amount of the national currency. For instance, if the foreign currency were Italian lire, with currently about 2,300 lire to the pound sterling, the FC1,000,000 would be a negligible amount in sterling terms, but if there were a currency near to a one to one relationship against the pound (*e.g.* the Irish pound) or even less, the amounts would be more substantial in real terms.

However, for the purposes of this example, let us assume that the foreign currency units do not represent a large domestic equivalent when converted, in which case, unless unfavourable movements in the interest rate structures are anticipated, the risk of incurring a loss against the spot/forward and forward/forward positions is minimal. In effect, as FC500,000 for five months is really the same as FC2,500,000 for one month, the real gap exposure is only FC1,500,000 for one month when the one month reverse gap is deducted from the five months' exposure converted into a one month equivalent. This interpretation of forward risk puts it into a more acceptable framework, although it ignores the fact that these transactions may not be covered at the same time.

By leaving all the forward exposures unmatched the dealer has also saved on the number of transactions to be processed, which is an important consideration. As the market does not really offer a service in outright forward cover, he would have had to engage in at least seven exchange deals to ensure satisfactory cover immediately, that is, three spot outright deals and two swaps. However, by postponing the decision until the end of the day, he is in a position to undo the gaps by executing one spot forward swap and another forward/forward deal – a total of four deals. In reality many more transactions might have to be engaged in if the dealer had instructions from his senior management to cover every exchange exposure, large or small, immediately. It would, of course, be unwise to restrict a dealer's actions by concentrating on limiting the number of transactions; that would be just as wrong as to ignore the cost of settling individual deals.

If he decided to leave the forward gaps open, given he is certain in his own mind that forward margins will not move dramatically in his disfavour, the dealer can then use these gaps the following day to make competitive quotations on one side of the market. In a way he has taken a two-way bet; he can even be aggressively competitive on both sides of the market as he can off-set one of the forward legs against whatever deal he transacts later on. Without such a forward book the dealer is hamstrung. He has to rely completely on market prices, and he may still have to open gaps, if his customers' deals cannot be undone in the market. Regretfully, when a dealer has an unfavourable position, whether a forward or a spot one, the tendency is for this individual to base his prices to the commercial clientele on the make up of these open positions, rather than on what the market says. This can result in business being lost and the customers feeling slighted if they find that other market-makers are in a position to quote more acceptable rates.

Obviously whatever the dealer does with his professional counterparts, he must be influenced by underlying positions, but the same considerations should not apply when quoting to commercial users. Even if a commercial user wishes to transact business *contra* to the dealer's interests, the price should be based on current market trends; the dealer should open forward gaps if necessary unless, of course, the amounts and the duration of the swap exceed the bounds of prudent banking.

It may be a valid opinion that based on the law of averages over a number of transactions and a period of time, amounts and maturity dates will come roughly into equilibrium. In practice, this situation rarely arises. A currency is seldom in a supply and demand equilibrium. There will nearly always be a clear trend. Country A exports more than Country B imports from Country

A, and in consequence, either the currency of Country A will have to appreciate or that of Country B depreciate. And if the situation of Country B *vis-à-vis* A also applies in its trading relationships with other countries, it is very likely that not only the exchange rate will depreciate but that the operative interest rates for the currency of Country B will rise. Trade is only one aspect that affects the value of a currency, capital in- or outflows can have a more immediate impact in the short run.

On a minute by minute basis, the dealer may not be aware of his exact forward positions, particularly those created by other departments in the bank, and before the introduction of computers in the dealing rooms, this information time-lag made it necessary for dealers to anticipate customer demand or supply. Fortunately, the advent of increasingly volatile exchange and interest rates has coincided with the installation of on-line terminals and video display units in the trading rooms, making it easier to input trans-actions and update positions instantly.

Spot transactions in cross currencies, which may be the preserve of different operators in a dealing room, can cause reporting difficulties and dilemmas when trying to allocate profits to the appropriate desk or unit. This problem is compounded in forward dealing, in view of the fact that at least one of the currencies will show a different forward amount from its spot transaction. The revaluation of forward positions and gaps in such a manner that both risk and performance evaluation are equitably allocated, constantly leads to acrimony between accountants and auditors on the one hand and dealers on the other. Even the most sophisticated hard and software has built-in disadvantages, and while small improvements in the revaluation system of an organization can iron out current distortions, it is quite often discovered at a later date that a change in dealing postures has opened up another weakness, sometimes due to previous improvements in the system.

It would seem that the only solution lies in splitting up the transactions right at the outset into their component parts, as will be explained in greater detail in the Chapter 13, Revaluation, and separating dealing room responsi-bilities in the same manner. Even if this means that some individuals will have to wear 'two hats', whatever the revaluation procedures adopted, foreign exchange managers and chief dealers should be more concerned with the actual dealing results, in spite of the fact that they may not show up at once because of the accounting standards applied. Naturally, they cannot completely ignore operational aspects, as some revaluation procedures can have an impact on results in the following accounting period, or even in ensuing financial years.

Advantages and Disadvantages of Forward Dealing

As pointed out previously, good spot dealers do not necessarily make good forward dealers. Spot dealing requires constant awareness of changing supply and demand situations, and pre-emptive action has to be taken all the time to protect underlying positions by realizing losses or profits. As the saying goes, 'the first loss is always the smallest'. This is very much a saying and does not hold true in all situations. Forward dealers acting in the same manner as spot operators would build up enormous forward positions and gaps and to some extent would lose control of their positions, especially with limits of all kinds imposed on the forward dealers: spot, settlement, gap, country, overall, intra-day. Though there is more room for manoeuvre in the forward market, there is less freedom to trade in and out of forward positions, contrary to the practice of spot traders. The spot dealer who trades one billion (1,000 million) for value spot knows that in two days' time the matched positions, though using up limits, will disappear when all parties effect settlements and restore his limits to their former totals. Limits in this context refer to the total exposure one bank is willing to incur with another for settlement risk, overall spot or forward exposure.

The forward dealer, on the other hand, who starts building up forward gaps will be blocking limits for months and sometimes years. The nearer he comes to the maturity dates of these forward positions, the more other inhibitions such as short-term settlement limits will affect the actions of his counterparties as well. It would be wrong to suppose that because one's own bank had a very generous limits policy, others apply the same generous criteria. By building up very large maturities with other banks in the near date values over a period of time, dealers can effectively make the name of their banks almost unacceptable in the market, and the fact that a name is 'under reference' does carry a cost.

Because of all the considerations that intrude on forward dealing, it can be a more demanding occupation than spot dealing, as the time it takes to build a position and bring it to a satisfactory conclusion takes far longer. A spot dealer knows the profit or loss or the risk potential of his position all the time if he keeps a running record and to some extent he could, if he wanted to, take remedial action immediately. Not so for the forward dealer. Apart from the usual limitations, the forward dealer has to monitor events and expectations. What will the balance of payments, retail price index, money supply, interest rates be like in three or six months' time? So, in essence, forward dealing is a question of taking strategic positions for long-term profit generation and tactical in and out trading using these strategic positions. Commercial banks with numerous customers may be forced to engage exclusively in forward dealing. But in any case, the dealer should be monitoring total outstandings and the length and magnitude of the forward gaps all the time. Only on a rare occasion is it justified to take a wholesale position in one maturity, and then only if the position is forced on the dealer as a result of a large and on the whole profitable relationship with a commercial customer or genuine correspondent of undoubted creditworthiness. However, in this situation it would be advisable to spread the risk by taking cover over several maturities to cut down on the time and margin exposure. For instance, if the client has executed a forward deal which does not fit the forward book of the dealer (for six months' settlement) then the dealer might be in a position to straddle the exposure by covering in the three and nine months' 'slots'. That is, of course, if he cannot unwind the six months' maturity because of the magnitude of the transaction.

The forward dealer is less exposed than the spot dealer, as forward rates normally move by fractions of one per cent per annum, instead of the one and two per cent nominal movements (and sometimes more) of the spot rates in the course of a dealing day. A forward dealer who loses one per cent per annum on a forward transaction for the one year has lost the same amount as a spot dealer who loses one per cent on a spot transaction. On an annual basis, the spot dealer would lose far more if he continued to lose one per cent nominally each day. A further advantage attached to forward dealing is that the trend of interest rate differentials is sometimes clearly charted, and consequently, a forward transaction executed in good time has an even chance of producing a profit. A 'plus' of forward position taking is that if the dealer knows that the odds are in favour of the interest rates of the respective currencies moving in a specific direction, he has more than an even chance. If only one of the anticipated interest rate movements occurs he is ensured of a profit.

Obviously, there is always a risk and however much a dealer is certain of events moving in his favour, they may take time to materialize. As in all forms of trading, for better or for worse, decisions have then to be made. Post-mortems usually show that the forward positions were taken too early and that action should have been delayed for a time. It is never easy to time actions. It is always either too late or too early, but the dealer who postpones decisions until the time seems to be ripe may never deal and as a result never make a loss; conversely he will never make a profit either. It is all too easy to miss the boat.

It is not always too late to join the bandwagon when a movement has just started, as long as available information and opinion confirms that the trend is firmly established. Naturally, delaying dealing decisions until a trend is firmly established also means giving up some of the profit potential and may also mean that the dealer who has dealt late must come out of the position at an earlier date, as his protective margin is insufficient to warrant waiting until the bitter end.

Forward Rates and Interest Differentials

In Chapter 3, Outright Forward Rates, it has already been explained that it is unusual for forward prices to be quoted as outright rates. It does happen in some countries where it is normal practice to do so. But most of the time forwards are priced as margins or spreads.

Slightly repetitive, but essential, is the statement that it is easier to consider the currency priced in terms of another as the currency that is at a premium or discount in the forwards. By standardizing thinking processes unfortunate misunderstandings will be avoided. For this reason, the fact that sterling is dealt in round amounts in dollar terms means that it is sterling that is at a premium or a discount, rather than the dollar in the forward market.

Most of the time the market-maker does not have to worry about how to establish a forward margin, market forces will do this for him. All he will have to do is to interpret the money markets and quote round, inside or close to the open market rates. At least, this is the case when a major currency is the subject of a forward quotation against another major currency. It is a different matter when a minor or exotic currency is being traded, then it will be vital for the dealer to know that the forward margin reflects the interest differentials, and if not, he will have to find out why there is a difference between the theoretical and actual rate. He may then find out that exchange regulations which mainly inhibit outflows (and more rarely, inflows, although sometimes both are affected) and the fact that the currency is not actively traded in the international market ensure that the market-makers in the particular currency can ignore interest rate parities in their calculations and simply base their prices on how much the market is prepared (and is sometimes forced) to pay.

Just as in spot transactions, the active forward markets are against the US dollar. It is possible that one day other currencies will acquire this iniquitous reserve currency status, but until that time it will be the US dollar providing the base for spot and forward dealing.

How to Establish the True Forward Margin

Theory and practice diverge on many occasions in all walks of life, and foreign exchange is no exception to this rule. Without a thorough grounding in the theory of a subject, practical aspects cannot be interpreted in a logical fashion. The theory of forward exchange must encompass the basic rule that the margins for forward transactions when linked to the effective interest rates for two currencies bring about interest rate parity. If the operative interest rates for US dollar and sterling are quoted at 10 per cent and 11 per cent per annum respectively, the cost or profit on the hedge from dollars into sterling, or the other way round, must negate the interest rate differential; in other words, the forward cost or profit must balance out the one per cent per annum differential.

That is the theory. Practice may upset this neat proposition simply because commercial organizations and banks have different funding costs and tax structures and consequently, varying interest arbitrage levels may prevail. Furthermore, at times the sheer bulk of forward operations may cause interest arbitrage opportunities to develop. This could happen when entrepreneurs want to acquire the currency of the country for purely speculative purposes and are not concerned about interest differentials.

Obviously, for a clearing bank in the United Kingdom with access to low cost sterling deposits the cost of generating sterling out of dollars may be too high, whereas the branch or subsidiary of an American bank in London may prefer to import funds from the United States and hedge them.

For commercial organizations the same rationale may apply, as effective interest rates vary considerably. The issuer of triple 'A' commercial paper in New York may have a low cost base and these funds could be used to fund the operations of a subsidiary in the UK. This may be cheaper than borrowing sterling from a bank in England. There are times that funds can flow freely from the US and though this facility may not be available at all times, other arbitrage opportunities then arise. Sometimes, it may well be possible to generate dollars for domestic usage out of the international market.

There are no hard and fast rules. However, the effective interest rates for wholesale transactions in the interbank market should still decide what the theoretical forward margins should be like. It is only when cheap sources of funds become available from other quarters, that the theoretical forward values take a back seat.

Extraneous events have an impact on effective interest rates, and sometimes cause them to move up or down. Nevertheless, their usefulness in calculating the optimum forward margins remains valid and essential as a base for discussion and computation. For further information *see also* Chapter 5.

5

INTEREST ARBITRAGE OPERATIONS

There are a number of ways in which dealers evaluate the percentage per annum of a forward rate and by adding and deducting this percentage from the interest differential establish whether interest arbitrage operations are profitable and feasible.

Definition of Interest Arbitrage between Two Currencies

Interest arbitrage between two currencies in its purest form consists of borrowing one currency and converting it into the other one, placing the proceeds in an investment for the period of the hedge and the borrowing, and, after taking out forward cover to protect the interest and swap differentials, showing a profit on the overall transaction.

Again the theory is simple, but practice does not always follow the principle to the letter. It must be said, that in some countries, particularly between Canada and the United States, fully hedged interest arbitrage operations occur every day and the intermediaries who produce these interest arbitrage packages take every exposure element into account. This is not unusual and frequently happens when a smaller country is to some extent economically dependent on a larger one, particularly if the smaller country has a greater need for liquidity than its larger neighbour.

Calculating the Interest Per Annum Using Forward Margins

The inappropriateness of some margin to interest rate conversions is best demonstrated by applying them to a hypothetical situation.

Example 5.1
   Assumptions:
   – Spot sterling/dollar $2.25 = £1.00
   – The effective interest rates for dollars are 10 per cent per annum and for sterling 11 per cent per annum.
   – A borrower in the United Kingdom has a need for £1,000,000

and decides to borrow US dollars instead of sterling and fully hedge the dollars into sterling.

Based on the approach that the percentage per annum differential is calculated on the spot rate and that for this transaction there is no loss or profit, the following results obtain: 1 per cent on the spot rate equals 2.25 ÷ 100 = 0.0225 or, if the spot rate is 2.25, the one year forward rate must be 2.2275.

But is this the right margin and does it produce the correct forward rate? To create £1,000,000 the borrower would have to acquire:

£1,000,000 × 2.25 = US$2,250,000.

$$£1,000,000 \text{ at } 11 \text{ per cent per annum} = \frac{£1,000,000 \times 11 \times 365}{365 \times 100} = £110,000$$

$$\$2,250,000 \text{ at } 10 \text{ per cent per annum} = \frac{\$2,250,000 \times 10 \times 365}{360 \times 100} = \$228,125$$

To cover the forward need of US$228,125 + US$2,250,000 should not require more than a payment of £110,000 + £1,000,000 and the outright rate to be achieved should not be worse than 2.232545 (*see* section, How to Calculate the Theoretical Forward Margin, page 51).

The assumption that the percentage of differential is based on the spot rate would result in a sizeable distortion, so that to repay US$2,478,125 at a rate of 2.25 − 0.0225 = 2.2275 would necessitate spending £1,112,514.03 to acquire the US dollar amount of $2,478,125.

Obviously, a discrepancy of this nature, other things being equal, could bring arbitrageurs, or other interested parties with a genuine need for dollars into the market. The reverse transaction, that is, borrowing sterling and converting this currency fully hedged into US dollars would produce a saving of roughly 0.25 per cent per annum. To a degree, market-makers ensure in their prices that if anybody is capable of engaging in interest arbitrage operations it must be the market-makers because that is the basis of their quotations. The thinking applied is 'if we cannot undo the deal in the exchange market, it must be possible to cover in the deposit market'.

Of course, there is the possibility that supply or demand for normal exchange cover could alter the one year forward to 220–215 or 230–225 or any other suitable margin which might make interest arbitrage a possible venture.

However, if there were ample supply or demand in the one year market this could have an impact on the spot rate, but this would only have a minor effect on the interest to be paid or received.

Example 5.1 should prove that the use of the spot rate is a certain way of getting the forward margin percentage wrong and could lead to such costly mistakes as $(0.0225 \times 100) \div 2.25 = 1$ per cent per annum, but really the 1 per cent interest differential in the interest rate structure should be represented by $2.25 - 2.232545 = 0.017455$ (normally forward margins are not quoted to this degree of exactness, as the general practice is to quote round the interest rate parity).

Another slightly more accurate way of computing the interest per annum as represented by the forward margins is to use the forward rate as the divider. For instance, the cost of converting dollars into sterling would then show as $(0.0225 \times 100) \div 2.2275 = 1.0101$ per cent per annum, but unfortunately, this approach also ignores the fact that interest and swap differentials will have to be covered to achieve perfect interest rate equilibrium. The percentage swap differential is accurate as far as it shows how much will have to paid for the dollars in one year's time just to buy back the principal, as US$2,250,000 $\div$ 2.2275 $=$ £1,010,101 and the extra sterling required compared to the converse spot transaction is £1,010,101 $=$ 1 per cent per annum.

Thus, the outright forward rate used as a divider does not provide the correct answer either. It merely evaluates the percentage per annum cost to hedge the spot amount, and even the introduction of differing days/year systems for dollars and sterling would not improve the situation substantially.

As previously pointed out (*see* page 48), there are few pure interest arbitrage opportunities, with the exception of currencies inhibited by exchange controls or an undeveloped money market. The original cost of the borrowing or the return on the investment decides whether the initiator of an interest arbitrage operation has a valid case. The entrepreneur must also be aware that the decision to cover or not to cover the interest element is a straight foreign exchange decision and should not form the basis for entering into an interest arbitrage transaction.

Although, for the sake of simplicity, one year examples have been used to prove the validity of most formulas, in a later example (*see* Example 5.6 on page 59) it will be shown that the principle of perfect interest arbitrage can be applied just as effectively to shorter- and longer-term transactions.

It does not matter really whether direct or indirect rates are used to gauge the profitability of an interest operation, as long as the optimum exchange rate produced is in the appropriate terms.

As for normal swap transactions, care must be taken with the spot rate used for the interest rate arbitrage transactions, as unfavourable rates when compounded over a number of operations can have a detrimental effect on cash-flows.

A partly hedged currency conversion, that is, one which does not allow for interest cover, will result in an outright exchange exposure which for revaluation purposes either will have to be amortized or left open to exchange rate fluctuations, thus making it difficult to judge the true profit or loss potential of such a transaction. This is another reason that, for accounting purposes, it is preferable to complete the circle by covering the hedge differential as well as the interest components.

In a dealing room split up for accounting and operational procedures into deposit and foreign exchange sides, the exposed interest element, if not fully covered, should be carried by the foreign exchange function as an open foreign exchange risk. Different considerations may prevail in a commercial organization with a limited number of interest arbitrage operations on the books, but the greater volume in the bank dealing rooms, and the constant in and out trading, make it essential to draw a clear line between true foreign exchange positions and savings generated out of lower borrowing costs or increased lending profits.

How to Calculate the Theoretical Forward Margin

Whereas in theory interest arbitrage operations should not be feasible, in practice other determinants can enter into the picture, creating opportunities for specialists in this field, as in the following cases.

a   Although the market quotes interest rates for standard borrowers and lenders, some borrowers do not enjoy the same creditworthiness status as others. Balance sheet considerations and geographical location are just two of the aspects that can result in higher or lower interest rates for borrowers.

b   The offered and bid interest rates or forward margins for particular maturities may be indicative and only arbitrageurs attuned to the conditions in a particular market and with established contacts and outlets, can take advantage of the situation. This applies mainly to minor and exotic currencies.

c   Foreign exchange controls and other regulatory constraints inhibit the actions of some market-makers and users, while others not restrained by these limitations are in a position to put these opportunities to profitable use.

d   Some borrowers and lenders are forced to take in funds or place deposits at unfavourable rates to protect illiquid or overliquid positions, and to cover these risks have to make their propositions overly attractive to more conservative or better placed operators.

But whatever the reasons, the interest arbitrageur or forward swap dealer has to be in a position to establish the true forward margin. To do this, no short cuts are possible, unless the market has been static over a period of time and the operator can calculate minor changes accurately without having to resort to detailed calculations. Timing is of the essence, as the opportunities presented may not be open for very long, particularly if the competition is more efficient in its calculations or relies on intuitive dealing. Intuitive dealing, though possibly the mainstay of straight swap transactions, is not something to be recommended when it comes to interest arbitrage transactions, as the latter use up asset and liability availability, contrary to swaps, which are off balance sheet.

To prove the validity of the exact forward equation, it is again necessary to go through a hypothetical transaction. In this instance, as the acceptance of the theory is all important, examples will be analysed of sterling/dollar and dollar/Deutsche Mark operations. The use of the two different currencies against US dollars is simply to demonstrate the importance of absolute accuracy and to highlight the effect widely varying interest rates can have on the outcome of a transaction.

Example 5.2

The spot rate for sterling/dollar is 2.2515 at a given time. This means that an arbitrageur who wishes to generate £1,000,000 would have to convert US$2,251,500 on the spot. If a further assumption is made that the effective interest rate for US dollars is 10 per cent per annum and for sterling 11 per cent per annum, these are all the ingredients needed to establish the theoretical forward rate and margin for sterling/dollar. Any divergence from this rate will create arbitrage opportunities as long as the favourable discrepancies are sufficient to cover the costs incurred in the various transactions and there is an adequate profit margin left over.

Assuming there are no interest rate differentials and the effective interest rates are at 'zero' and consequently, no forward premium or discount applies, the following results would be achieved:

	Borrow/Repay	US dollars	Swap	Sterling	Loan/Receive
Spot	$2,251,500	($2,251,500)		£1,000,000	($1,000,000)
3 Months	($2,251,500)	$2,251,500		(£1,000,000)	£1,000,000
	0	0		0	0

Either sterling or dollars could be converted immediately at the spot rate. This would also be the position for three months' transactions if all components are in absolute equilibrium.

Unfortunately exchange pressures, interest rate differentials and the length of a forward transaction may cause distortions, which is the time an interest arbitragist can take advantage.

Effect of the Interest Day Year

In the perfect market example above and in any theory of a perfectly balanced economy, one important element has been overlooked and that is the interest day year. The interest on sterling deposits and loans is calculated on the exact number of days, *i.e.* 365 (leap year 366) over 365, thus the yield on a one year loan or deposit equals exactly the per cent per annum quoted. The interest year for dollars, on the other hand, is the exact number of days over 360. Obviously, when interest rates for dollars rise to double digit figures, a dollar investment will earn interest for five more days than a sterling investment for a similar period. Consequently, whether the period of a loan is for one year, shorter or longer than one year, the fact that the 365 or 360 year basis will have to be employed in the interest formula will make a substantial difference to the swap prices. The standard formula for working out the interest is:

$$\frac{\text{Principal} \times \text{Rate} \times \text{Tenor (days)}}{360 \text{ (or 365)} \times 100} = \text{Interest}$$

or, applied to the above example (Example 5.2, page 52):

$$\frac{\$2,251,500 \times 10 \times 90}{360 \times 100} = \$56,287.50$$

and

$$\frac{£1,000,000 \times 11 \times 90}{365 \times 100} = £27,123.29$$

Having established the interest amounts for the dollar and sterling investments, the next stage of the reasoning can be looked at. Given that by now the reader has accepted the necessity that, in the theoretical forward rate, the interest element must be eliminated and that in theory interest arbitrage should not be possible, it becomes a simple matter to calculate the perfect forward rate under the above interest rate conditions.

Example 5.3

   The reasoning goes as follows. After three months the dollars have grown into $2,251,500 + $56,287.50 = $2,307,787.50 and whether the dollars are borrowed or lent they should be worth exactly the countervalue in sterling, plus interest, *i.e.* £1,000,000 + £27,123.29 = £1,027,123.29. And if the market reflects this perfect situation, the outright forward rate for sterling/dollar in the three months (in this example 90 days) should be 2,307,787.50 ÷ 1,027,123.29 = 2.246846. In consequence, the forward margin would have to be 2.2515 − 2.246846 = 0.004654. The market does not quote in this exact fashion, and very likely the quotation might have been 0.0046 or 0.00465, simplified to 46 or 46.5. Market operators are very much aware that 46 or 46.5 stand for so many basis points. A dealer who simply tried to convert this forward margin into percentage per annum would be bound to be wrong:

$$\frac{0.0046 \times 4 \times 100}{2.2515} = 0.817233 \text{ per cent per annum}$$

In his quest for simplification he has even ignored the fact that there are 365 days in a full year and that a more accurate computation would have allowed for this fact:

$$\frac{0.0046 \times 365 \times 100}{2.2515 \times 90} = 0.828584 \text{ per cent per annum}$$

but this is still well away from the 1 per cent differential. At these percentage levels a dealer might be tempted to borrow dollars and swap into sterling hoping to save or gain 0.17 per cent per annum.

The use of the forward rate would marginally improve the accuracy of the calculation as:

$$\frac{0.0046 \times 365 \times 100}{2.2469 \times 90} = 0.830280 \text{ per cent per annum}$$

but even this result is less than satisfactory.

The impact of duration and wide interest differentials can play havoc with the calculations and interpretations, as can be seen in the following dollar/Deutsche Mark example.

Example 5.4

Deutsche Marks can be borrowed for six months at 8 per cent per annum and when swapped into dollars can be invested at 14.5 per cent per annum for the same period of time. Although the interest years for dollars and Deutsche Marks (in the Euro-markets) are identical, 365 days over 360, this factor must still be taken into account when finding out the theoretical forward rate. The spot rate dollar/Deutsche Mark happens to be 2.00 which is rather handy for calculation purposes.

Just as for the sterling/dollar example (*see* Example 5.1, page 48), it is essential to work out interest payable and receivable and to treat the net results as balancing items to bring the whole transaction into equilibrium.

Thus:
$$\frac{DM2,000,000 \times 8 \times 182}{360 \times 100} = DM80,888.89$$

and
$$\frac{US\$1,000,000 \times 14.5 \times 182}{360 \times 100} = US\$73,305.56$$

Consequently, in six months' time DM2,080,888.89 should be worth US$1,073,305.56 and the outright forward rate must be 2,080,888.89 ÷ 1,073,305.56 = DM1.938767.

At this outright rate, it would not pay the arbitrageur to enter the market, as there would be no profit on the overall transaction. The forward margin would be 0.061233 or 0.0612, quoted as 612 or 613, but in any case this is not sufficient to permit interest arbitrage.

In this example, the spread for the period converted to percentage per annum might show a favourable interest arbitrage opportunity for the adventurous and careless, as:

$$\frac{0.0612 \times 365 \times 100}{2.00 \times 182} = 6.136813 \text{ per cent per annum}$$

Or, on the face of it a clear profit margin of $14.5 - (8 + 6.1368) = 0.3632$ per cent per annum using the spot rate.

The use of the forward rate would improve this inaccurate result dramatically, but would still leave a substantial margin for error, as:

$$\frac{0.0612 \times 365 \times 100}{1.938767 \times 182} = 6.330635 \text{ per cent}$$

showing a profit margin of approximately 0.16 per cent per annum, which also proves that the longer the period and the wider the interest differential, the more appropriate the use of the forward rate becomes, although still inaccurate when applied to interest arbitrage transactions.

Putting this example in a full year context based on the same rates, the result is:

$$\frac{DM2,000,000 \times 365 \times 8}{360 \times 100} = DM162,222.22$$

$$\frac{US\$1,000,000 \times 365 \times 14.5}{360 \times 100} = US\$147,013.89$$

And the outright forward rate would work out to DM2,162,222.22 ÷ US$1,147,013.89 = DM1.885088, or a margin of 0.1149 or 1149.

The percentage per annum represented by 1149 worked over the spot rate would produce a favourable discrepancy of:

$$\frac{0.1149 \times 100}{2.00} = 5.745 \text{ per cent per annum}$$

or a profit margin of 0.75 per cent per annum. This would represent quite a substantial profit margin or cost saving if the interest element were excluded from the calculation, in other words, not covered in the forward market. Also, as the example covers a whole year period, there is no need to use the exact number of days, as a swap made for a year has no further days' adjustments in it. In examples for three and six months' operations (such as this example and *Example* 5.3) it is essential to include the exact number of days over or under 365 days, as the dealer would have to continue the swap operation for the whole period to annualize the swap cost or profit.

Again the application of the outright forward rate will narrow the distortion considerably:

$$\frac{0.1149 \times 100}{1.885088} = 6.095206 \text{ per cent per annum}$$

leaving a profit margin of 0.4047 per cent per annum. This distortion in the computations is too large, as the favourable margin of this dimension would attract arbitrageurs in droves.

Unless there is a regulatory constraint or similar inhibition, it is most unlikely that profit opportunities of this magnitude would occur in a stable market. Of course, they are bound to arise in unstable conditions but then they may disappear just as quickly as market forces bring the component parts back into equilibrium.

It is possible to construct tables enabling the checking of forward rates in terms of percentage per annum at a glance, but they would be cumbersome, as there are four variables: the two interest rates; the period; and last, but not least, the spot rate. And to calculate the effectiveness of forward rates for longer than one year would involve considerations such as compound interest and taxation, as will be shown later in this chapter (*see* page 62).

Covering Exchange Exposures

Interest arbitrageurs could argue that as long as there is sufficient cash-flow in the currency in which the interest has to be covered, there is no exchange risk. This is true in terms of absolute exchange exposure, but to put this proposition into practice might mean that favourable opportunities to sell forward receivables at a premium would have to be abandoned. On the other hand, to state that the interest element should never be left exposed would be wrong as well. But decisions to leave the interest or for that matter, the swap differential, exposed must always be based on pure exchange rate considerations and should be carried on the foreign exchange books rather than in a separate interest arbitrage account.

Though deliberate decisions can be taken whether or not to cover the interest and swap differential, the principle of establishing the ideal forward rate remains the same. It is only once the perfect forward rate has been established that rational judgements can be made; whether to enter into a deal, or to go for straightforward deposits or loans in a particular currency without the encumbrance of an interest arbitrage operation.

Calculating the Exact Forward Rate

The formula to establish the exact forward rate based on effective interest rates is really an extension of the normal interest calculations. The simplest and easiest way to accomplish this feat is to use the spot rate as explained in the following example.

Example 5.5

The spot sterling rate is at a given time 2.2515 and the effective interest rates for dollars and sterling 10 and 11 per cent per annum respectively. Thus:

$$2.2515 + \left(\frac{2.2515 \times 10 \times 90}{360 \times 100} \right) = 2.3077875$$

$$1 + \left(\frac{1 \times 11 \times 90}{365 \times 100} \right) = 1.0271232$$

$$2.3077875 \div 1.0271232 = 2.246845$$

As long as the dealer knows the operative interest rates, he can work out the forward rate at which the transaction breaks even and how much more he would need to make it worthwhile. The problem still remains of how to compute what a forward rate represents in percentage per annum. But before turning to this question, it may be advisable to put the equation to establish the perfect forward rate in an easy to apply formula. The only time the equation can be simplified is when the one year basis is 365 for both currencies. Otherwise, for the sake of accuracy, the day element will have to be included.

Consequently, the exact forward rate must always be the result of the following reasoning: the spot rate for one unit (or round amount) of Unit B priced in terms of Currency A will form the basis of the first interest calculation using the spot rate.

(*a*) Spot rate for Currency B $+ \left(\dfrac{\text{Spot rate for B} \times \text{Rate} \times \text{Tenor (days)}}{360 \times 100 \text{ (or } 365 \times 100)} \right)$

(*b*) One unit (or round amount) of B $+ \left(\dfrac{\text{One unit of B} \times \text{Rate} \times \text{Tenor (days)}}{360 \times 100 \text{ (or } 365 \times 100)} \right)$

$$\frac{\text{Result of } (a)}{\text{Result of } (b)} = \text{Outright forward rate}$$

The difference between the spot and the outright forward rate represents the forward margin.

Obtaining an Exact Percentage Per Annum

To convert the forward margin into an exact percentage per annum still creates a problem as in Example 5.5 (page 57) when using the spot rate and even allowing for the annualization of the years would produce:

$$\frac{0.00465 \times 365 \times 100}{2.2515 \times 90} = 0.837589 \text{ per cent per annum}$$

The formula which shows the exact percentage per annum difference of a forward margin is rather complicated and the use of programmable calculators is a definite advantage. The formula reads:

$$\frac{\dfrac{360}{\text{No. of days}} + \dfrac{\text{Rate for valued currency}}{100}}{\text{Spot} \times 100} \times \text{Forward premium/discount}$$

or, applied to the US dollar/Deutsche Mark example (*see* Example 5.4, page 54) for six months (182 days):

$$\frac{\dfrac{360}{182} + \dfrac{14.5}{100}}{2.00 \times 100} \times 612 = \frac{2.123022}{200} \times 612$$

$$= 6.4964447 \text{ per cent per annum}$$

As US dollars yield 14.5 per cent per annum and the conversion of Deutsche Marks to US dollars costs 8 per cent per annum + 6.496447 per cent per annum = 14.496447 per cent per annum there is no profit (or loss) and no valid reason to effect an interest arbitrage operation. The marginal difference of 0.0035 per cent per annum is caused by the application of 612 instead of 612.33.

Naturally, a holder of Deutsche Marks liquid assets with a financing need in US dollars may well decide to convert at the break-even point, but obviously he does not mean to engage in interest arbitrage. It is more convenient for him to limit the creation of unnecessary assets, as otherwise he would have to place the Deutsche Marks and would still have to borrow US dollars.

Positive Interest Arbitrage

Fully hedged profitable interest arbitrage operations are rarely feasible in a free and open market but allowance must be made for the fact that there is more than one arbitrage level.

A slightly more sophisticated form of interest arbitrage, which does not quite meet the theoretical arbitrage criteria, is the positive interest arbitrage transaction. By taking calculated risks and generating front-end profits (it is inadvisable to take front-end losses), traders either can improve the performance of their assets or switch to a different source of funds. As 'sure-fire' profit opportunities very seldom present themselves, the dealer is forced 'willy-nilly' to engage in exposed liquidity positions. As a matter of fact, the main skill required from a dealer is the ability to limit the risk element, to anticipate events and to achieve favourable results by juggling with exposures.

Example 5.6

Let us assume that a bank placed a US dollar deposit for three months and earned 9 per cent per annum on this investment. Unfortunately, just after the deposit was placed the interest rates moved the wrong way, *i.e.* they moved up, and to take in a matching deposit in time and amount would involve taking an outright loss of 0.25 per cent per annum. In other words, the cost of three months' dollar deposits has gone up to 9.25 per cent per annum. The one month and two month rates have also risen in sympathy to 9 per cent per annum which would mean that if the operator covered the three months' liquidity exposure with one or two months' money he would make a slight loss on a compound interest basis.

Given the operator is reasonably certain that interest rates have nearly reached their peak, he would hesitate to take funds for longer than three months, for which he might have to pay 9–9.375 per cent per annum. Naturally, if he anticipated another jump he would have no doubt about his actions: he would take funds for a longer period, incur the loss on the near side in the hope of recouping this loss when he puts out in due course the forward/forward funds. He would try to make good on the swings what he lost on the roundabouts.

But if the dealer felt that the rates were on a plateau, he would look around for ways of funding this exposure at a profit margin. Being an experienced dealer, he would know that perfect interest arbitrage hardly ever exists and that, in any case, it would not be worth his while to go through a number of transactions to save a marginal amount. Having put himself into a difficult situation, he wants to prove his dealing competence by turning a loss into a profit. One possibility that sometimes exists is to borrow other currencies for shorter maturities than the lending period and to swap these funds into a forward maturity which does not necessarily match the original borrowing.

Looking around the market for suitable currencies, the dealer finds that Swiss francs are on offer at 4 per cent in the three months and that when this rate is added to the swap cost, dollars can be produced at a little more than 9.25 per cent per annum. It would, of course, be ridiculous to create dollars in this way when they can be obtained in a straightforward manner at 9.25 per cent per annum.

However, say he notices that one month Swiss francs are offered at 3 per cent per annum and a stable exchange rate is forecast for Swiss francs and that there is a possibility that Swiss interest rates may come down, with the odds strongly against a rise. This is the kind of opportunity a real arbitrage dealer dreams about. Instead of making a loss of 0.25 per cent per annum, he finds himself with a chance of funding the placement at 8–8.25 per cent per annum. Arriving at 8–8.25 per cent per annum as the rate is simply a question of instinctively knowing that if three months' dollars cost 9.25 per cent and three months' Swiss francs cost 4 per cent, the swap differential must be approximately 5.25 per cent per annum. By borrowing Swiss francs for one month and executing a swap for three months, at least for the first month the cost of the dollar funds will be only 3 per cent per annum + 5.25 per cent per annum = 8.25 per cent per annum – give or take a slight swap margin and the compounding effect of borrowing Swiss francs for one month at a time and having to carry the interest until maturity. However, at 3 per cent per annum the compounding effect is insignificant for that short period of time.

And even if Swiss franc interest rates moved to 4 per cent per annum, when he rolls the deposit in one month's time, he would still gain on the overall transaction, as 3 + 4 + 4 = 11 ÷ 3 = 3.666 per cent per annum. Thus the overall cost of funding the three months' dollars will still only work out to 3.666 + 5.25 = 8.916 per cent per annum, still leaving a small profit margin. Looking at what the potential loss could have been, the dealer has saved his bank approximately 0.33 per cent per annum.

Regrettably, this type of interest arbitrage situation does not offer itself all the time. It is a question of monitoring distortions in the yield curves for particular currencies and evaluating the possibility that the discrepancy reflects the future trend of interest rates. For instance, if the 4 per cent per annum rate for the three months' maturity indicated that the market felt that Swiss rates had to increase, it would have been unwise to enter into this operation.

Every positive approach to a particular foreign exchange or funding transaction has its drawbacks. Split level interest arbitrage is a very difficult operation to identify and quantify on a bank's books. It is nearly impossible to tie the loose ends together. Was the Swiss francs conversion to dollars an exchange transaction or a deposit deal?

This case illustrates the need to separate deposit and foreign exchange functions for profit analysis and accounting purposes. After all, the gap exposure of the one against the three months' dollar placement has no visible link with the spot against the three months' Swiss franc gap and the one month Swiss francs deposit. The solution would seem to lie in passing internal contracts between the deposit and foreign exchange desks, in other words, covering the exchange aspect in the foreign exchange side and leaving the deposit desk to cope with the one month to three months' Swiss francs gap position. There is also, of course, a one to three months' gap in US dollars, but both the dollar and Swiss franc gaps are merely interest exposures not exchange ones. The problem is that, unless this accounting separation is implemented, the Swiss francs gap exposure can be undone in the exchange markets, thus negating the original plan to create cheaper dollars.

Levels of Interest Arbitrage

One man's interest arbitrage is another man's loss. There are differing levels of interest rates which can make conversion of one currency into another for funding purposes either a cost saver or a genuine profit opportunity. An issuer of commercial paper in New York may find that the cost of borrowing domestic US dollars is lower than the effective interest rate in the international market. Hence, by hedging into sterling or other suitable currency, he can make a clear profit, whereas these funds invested in the domestic US market would not offer profit opportunities for matched lending. This is one of the reasons causing arbitrage levels to move away from their true equilibrium. Funds suddenly become available in one centre and find their way into the international arena. For instance, a US multinational company with a subsidiary in the United Kingdom might find it more advantageous to use funds surplus to requirement in the United States to fund the activities of its subsidiary in the United Kingdom, especially as the full hedge covering interest as well as the normal swap differential make the US origin funds cheaper than borrowing in the United Kingdom money market. It is also easier to transfer funds in this manner than to establish a domestic UK bank line and, furthermore, the US multinational corporation saves the profit spread the UK bank might add to the basic cost of the funds. In principle, this fully hedged transfer from the United States to Britain meets the interest arbitrage requirements of leaving no exchange exposure.

If other US interests then became aware of the savings that can be realized by engaging in funding swaps, their activities might have impact on the forward rates and yields obtainable in the international market, and bring domestic and international dollar interest rates into balance.

Interest Arbitrage for Periods in Excess of One Year

From every aspect, interest arbitrage operations for periods in excess of one year – particularly for longer than two years – create complications which cannot always be accurately quantified or evaluated. Whether these long-term – in the foreign exchange sense – operations are really profitable is a matter of careful analysis of all the factors involved: compound interest, taxation, remittance of dividends to the shareholders or parent company, and the currency in which the earnings are generated. For instance, if a transaction straddles two tax or financial years, the remittance of profits and payment of taxes could mean that the favourable cash-flow, which produced the extra profits and in itself made the operation viable, disappears. And as a result, the following years could show losses. This makes it vital that from the outset the calculations allow for detrimental tax and financial implications to ensure that the outstanding periods remain profitable in themselves. The evaluation of tax and other complications is not easy to accomplish.

During the years of exchange control in the United Kingdom, there were frequently opportunities to borrow US dollars or other suitable Euro-currencies in excess of one year. These funds could then be converted into sterling for on-lending to local authorities (UK municipalities) at fixed rates or sometimes at rates which increased over the life-time of the loan. Although these transactions were only entered into when they showed a net profit without covering the interest element, the main reason for these propositions being so attractive was that they created a pool of exchange sterling which could be reversed over the exchanges into the external (also called Euro-sterling) market. The reversal took place whenever domestic rates were lower than the yields obtainable in the external market for sterling. An interesting factor was that because reversal was anticipated, it made little sense to cover the interest element, as the reversal produced a favourable currency income.

The above sterling interest arbitrage operations were an exception to the general rule that interest must be covered at all times. But flexibility must be the guiding principle in forward and interest arbitrage dealing, otherwise profit situations could be missed altogether.

It is customary for swaps and deposits under one year to ignore interim interest payments on placements or loans unless they affect the outcome of a transaction detrimentally, or improve on the results substantially. Naturally, when periods in excess of one year are considered, the implications of interim – usually annual – interest payments must be taken into account, as the swap transaction will be for two or three years and longer. If the funds generated are used to make a loan to a commercial borrower, it will be very likely that the beneficiary of the loan will have to settle interest bi-annually and sometimes quarterly. And the compounding effect, when interest rates are in double digits, will be very favourable to the bank granting the loan. It is the compounding element that sweetens the concoction. If the interest rate on the borrowing is lower than the rate applied to the loan, it is perfectly valid to assume that the cash-flow can be invested at some profit, but at the same time, it would be quite wrong to take the view that this can be done at the original favourable rate. That would be too optimistic and would not allow for interest rate fluctuations which are bound to happen over a three year life span.

It would be wiser to assume that no benefits will accrue from the favourable interest flows, as these may be negated by taxation and dividends. A completely negative attitude to loans and deposits in excess of one year would be wrong as well, as otherwise lending and borrowing for these longer periods would cease altogether. But as long as realistic attitudes and a healthy degree of pessimism as to the usage that eventually will be made of the cash-flow prevails, dealers will not be drawn to hasty conclusions and will only engage in these longer-term operations after careful analysis of advantages and drawbacks.

The above was just a short explanation of some of the factors that must be considered when judging the merits of a proposal to borrow and invest funds in different currencies on a fully hedged basis for longer than one year. Granted that the tax and dividend problems are not easy to solve, as dividends are almost never paid until well after the end of the financial year and, unless the authorities are very efficient (tax can take a year or two before it is claimed), the overall result may still be positive if there is an ample profit margin on the transaction. Whatever the circumstances, it still remains just as important for the basic components of an interest arbitrage transaction when fully hedged not to show a loss from the outset. And the theoretical forward rate should form the basis of whether to engage in a longer-term arbitrage transaction.

The main components of a viable model to check the accuracy of and profitability of a forward rate for two or three years' maturity are the following:

a   that interest will be paid and received annually and will be (or may have to be) covered in the forward market for each maturity until the final date.

b   that negative interest differentials will have to be carried for the life-time of the transaction. *Positive interest differentials will not be available in full and though the model will allow for the fact that they are available in practice, any party engaging in longer-term interest arbitrage must calculate the impact of non-availability once the theoretical forward rate has been established.*

c   the theoretical forward market must cover all the known risks. Naturally, unless the forward margin allows for a profit there is little point in dealing except if other considerations, such as reverse swaps, enter into the picture.

Interest Arbitrage in the Medium Term

Just as for shorter and up to one year swaps, the medium-term forward rates do not always reflect the interest rate equilibrium and the divergence from equilibrium may be more pronounced than for shorter maturities, as fewer market-makers operate in this segment of the forward market. Also, amounts and names will be subject to more intense scrutiny. In a way, there is no real market in the medium term, wheeling and dealing is out of the question and negotiation is a more accurate description of the posturing of users and market-makers. Sometimes these negotiations are of a protracted nature.

From the market-maker's point of view – that is, the dealer providing the forward quotations – it is absolutely essential that he can work out the theoretical rate with near accuracy. The forward market-maker is not concerned with interest arbitrage, he is more interested in undoing any exposures he incurs at a profit as soon as possible, though interest rates provide the components for fixing the break-even outright forward rate and consequentially, the exact forward margin. It may take some time to accomplish this, but the intention is there from the beginning, unless he has an existing gap exposure in the same time slot. There may be times that the forward market-maker will base his quotations and positions on anticipated interest rate movements in preference to extant forward rates. This kind of strategic forward gap creation is more active at times of extreme currency crisis than in periods of stability. It is also quite possible that in times of crisis only one-way prices will be available. In other words, there will be more buyers than sellers or vice versa.

Obviously, in a crisis, interest rates for medium-term periods will not make the same impact as exchange exposure considerations. Conversely, in stable times the interest rates will provide the basis for the exact margins a market-maker needs to create an active market. As is the case for shorter maturities, the forward margins will normally be around the interest rate equilibrium point. It would be wrong to assume that market-makers agonize all the time about the interest rate arbitrage factor. Many times their quotations are based on the margins quoted by the competition. This is the time that distortions can arise and the interest rate arbitrageur comes into his own.

The exact forward margin can be established in two ways. Either the interest amounts in the two currencies will be covered in the exchange market for their settlement day, or (a more satisfactory approach) the interest amounts will have to be carried until the final maturity. In the first instance implied forward rates will have to be used for the annual interest settlements and even then some allowance will have to be made for the profit margin which produces a favourable cash-flow. Rather than using unwieldy 'odd exchange rates', in the following example the carry forward approach has been adopted. To simplify the computations it is assumed that US$2 = £1.

Example 5.7

A bank wishes to establish the perfect forward rate for borrowing sterling through dollars for a period of two years. The amount the bank wishes to generate is £1,000,000 and consequently, the dollar equivalent must be US$2,000,000 on the spot. The effective interest rates for sterling and dollars are 10 per cent and 11 per cent per annum respectively for all the intervening periods as well as the two year maturity, thus permitting the reinvestment of surplus funds or borrowing of shortfalls at the same rates. To cover a three year transaction would add very little to the principle. It would only mean extending the operation for another year. Obviously, if the dealer anticipated interest changes in one year's time, he would have to allow for this fact in his calculations.

At the first anniversary of the loan and deposit, the respective currencies will be worth:

$$\frac{£1,000,000 \times 11}{100} = £110,000 = £1,110,000$$

and the dollars

$$\frac{\$2,000,000 \times 10 \times 365}{360 \times 100} = \$202,777.78 = \$2,202,777.78$$

and if these amounts carried for another year, the result will be:

$$\frac{£1,110,000 \times 11}{100} = £122,100 = £1,232,100$$

and for dollars

$$\frac{\$2,202,777.78 \times 10 \times 365}{360 \times 100} = \$223,337.19 = US\$2,426,114.97$$

And consequently, the outright rate for two year sterling/dollar should be 2,426,114.97 ÷ 1,232,100 = 1.96909 and the margin would be quoted as 0.03091 or in market terms 309.

It would be quite wrong for the arbitrageur to take the view that after one year only £890,000 has to be borrowed to finance the loan. That would be a mistake, as £1,000,000 had been lent originally and generated through dollars, thus, the surplus has to be placed in the market place. And it makes no difference whether the interest arbitrageur is constantly borrowing and lending in the currencies and consequently diminishing or increasing the cash-flow. He would still have to look at each transaction in isolation, as they are, in theory at least, self-liquidating. Again, if the interest element were ignored, this would improve the situation, as the forward rate and spread would then leave a significant profit margin in sterling. Of course, what would happen in one and two years' time when the dollar interest has to be covered in the exchange market is another matter.

If the position had been taken that the interest would have to be covered in the exchange market, this would not have changed the underlying calculations much because the theoretical rate for one year would have to reflect the interest differential for one year and the favourable interest flow reinvested.

To make Example 5.7 easier to understand, a simple exchange rate and relatively straightforward interest rates have been used. What the operator may have to do in practice is to adjust the calculations to allow for the fact that in one year (or two or three) interest rates may have moved up or down and that these adjustments may make his transaction less viable.

General Comments

As repeatedly pointed out in this chapter, reality and theory rarely coincide, and it is up to the traders to find out the reasons why they do not. Though there may be a divergence in the market structure, it is essential to establish the theoretical forward value of a currency, to ensure that at a later date no inexplicable unfavourable results come to the fore.

In the haste of making rather complicated calculations, the annual results of a transaction can be reversed. Although a sterling/dollar dealer in London would be familiar enough with the way the results of a sterling/dollar operation should be calculated, the same consideration may not apply when he is trying to accomplish the same feat between, let us say, Danish Kroner and French francs. The simplest way round this problem is to divide the currency in which a quotation is made by the currency that is being priced. For instance, if so many French francs have to be paid to acquire Danish Kroner 100, the rate is in French franc terms; then it is the French francs that will have to be divided by the Danish Kroner result, and vice versa.

For the professional trader, interest arbitrage and its more sophisticated progeny positive interest arbitrage are, from a purely technical point of view, the most challenging and rewarding, both intellectually and in terms of profitability.

6

SPOT AND FORWARD DATES

Most readers of this book will already have a thorough grounding in the way maturity (value, settlement, forward) dates of exchange contracts are determined. The principles are fairly straightforward, but in many situations the finer points can result in misunderstandings.

Definition

The spot, cash, forward, value, maturity, settlement day of an exchange contract is the day on which the contracting parties (2) pay and receive the currencies (2) which are being bought or sold.

The term 'cash' usually refers to an exchange transaction contracted for settlement on the day the deal is negotiated. This term is mainly used in the North American markets and those countries which rely for foreign exchange services on these markets because of time zone preference. In Europe and the markets to the east, cash transactions would normally be referred to as value same day deals.

Spot Dates

As most major money centres and most major currencies are based on the spot principle, the spot date is the settlement day which also coincides with the exchange rate for a currency.

Thus, the spot rate for dollars against sterling in London is also the current exchange rate, and although during the course of the dealing day this rate will fluctuate, subject to supply and demand, at some time in the day the quoted spot rate will be the one used by the financial papers to evaluate the strength of the dollar and sterling in relation to each other. Similarly, the spot rate for the dollar in Frankfurt or the spot rate for Deutsche Marks in Paris will be the exchange rates for these currencies.

Fixing the Spot Date

The importance of fixing the exact spot date or for that matter any settlement date lies in the necessity for parties to an exchange transaction to know the day on which they will have to exchange currencies in final settlement of their contract.

Example 6.1

If a bank in London sells £1,000,000 to a bank in New York and the rate is fixed at 2.25 (US$2.25) per pound sterling, then on the spot date the bank in London will have to pay £1,000,000 to whomever the New York bank uses as its correspondent in London. This correspondent bank could very well be the London bank which was party to the transaction. In return, the London bank would receive US$2,250,000 in New York.

But how to fix the spot date? The operative principle is simply that if one party contacts another and requests a firm quotation (the price at which the quoting party is willing to execute a deal for a reasonable amount) for spot settlement, the quoting bank's spot date is the one which will be applied, if no specific mention of a preferential date is made before the deal is struck. In this example, the spot date would be two days hence, and this day would have to coincide with an open, banking, business day in both centres, London and New York, thus making it possible (at least, theoretically) for the exchange of the currencies to take place simultaneously. Simplicity itself, as long as the business or banking days can be clearly established.

Thus, given there are no intervening holidays in either country and a bargain is struck on a Friday, the spot date falls on the following Tuesday. Problems immediately arise when the Monday falls on a bank holiday in New York, but only if the London bank had contacted the New York bank. If the Monday had been a holiday in New York and the London bank had either forgotten this fact or simply overlooked it, then the New York bank would have applied the New York spot date which could be the following Wednesday and not the Tuesday. The London dealer would naturally take it for granted that the New York dealer had applied value Tuesday as this was the spot date in London. On the Tuesday the London bank would have paid £1,000,000 expecting to receive the dollar equivalent in New York, but would have found out when it was too late that the New York bank would only remit the dollars on Wednesday.

Naturally, professional dealers would rarely make this kind of unforgivable error, especially when banks in major centres are operating in each other's currencies. However, the situation is less clear when the currency (or currencies) is that (or are those) of a minor or exotic country because then the banking holiday calendar may not be as well-known and sometimes holidays are created without prior notice. But even in the case of lesser currencies, it would be crass negligence on the part of the dealer not to mention his preferred settlement date before requesting a quotation and at some time during the exchange of details this value date must be stated to ensure that there is no possibility of misunderstanding.

The position would have been quite different if the New York bank had contacted London for quotations, because then the settlement date would have been based on the London calendar. Although, the Monday might well have been a holiday in New York, as long as it was a banking day in London, the Tuesday would have been the spot day. Thus, it is the business banking days in the country of the bank providing quotations which determine the spot date. The enquirer is the party who must make sure that his spot day coincides with the one applied by the respondent.

From time to time, even established markets diverge from the spot date principle for practical reasons. Usually this happens when the calendar is filled with non-banking days and other technical features such as the year end intrude on a normally clear-cut situation. Then, though the theoretical spot date may still exist, banks only quote for the first business day they consider free from extraneous pressures and for which an orderly market exists. In effect, that day then really becomes the spot day, as nearer value dates will be based on the rates quoted for the optimum settlement day.

In most dealing rooms the appropriate spot and forward dates for all major currencies are collated every morning and in some of the more efficient, or less busy, rooms the night before. The dates are established and later checked with other participants in the market, particularly with the brokers, for accuracy and effectiveness.

As mentioned in the sterling/dollar example (Example 6.1, page 68), the exact value date or spot date are of utmost importance in foreign exchange transactions. Naturally, the correct value date is always important because the foreign exchange market operates on the compensated value (*valeur compensée*) principle, which ensures that neither party to an exchange operation extends credit to the other one. That means that the day the London bank pays the sterling amount the American bank has to remit the dollar equivalent. With all the good-will in the world, it must be obvious that it would be impossible to ensure that both payments reach the respective beneficiaries simultaneously. With a time difference of five hours (sometimes six), London banks close for clearing about the time New York banks open their doors. Consequently, the London bank will have to provide the New York bank with an intraday overdraft. Fortunately, in the developed money markets, interest is only charged for overnight overdrafts, and there is no intraday interest rate charged. One could imagine that if one day interest rates reached astronomical levels intraday overdrafts might be charged as well, particularly if the high interest rates were a reflection of possibly higher inflation levels. Developments in electronic banking may eventually assure both parties to a transaction that their respective input into a sophisticated clearing system will tally. Neither party would then be exposed, as even across different time zones clearing would take place at the push of a button.

Suggestions of how to overcome the time zone differential of spot and forward dates abound, but the lack of agreement among the thousands of banks which would have to take part in an instantaneous clearing system make it an impracticable proposition for the time being. However, if the exact spot date principle could be made to include the exact time of settlement on that day, whether with different time zones or not, this would increase the dealing potential in the market, as well as lessen the impact of credit and limit considerations which always enter into exchange transactions. If a large creditworthy market-maker were assured that a smaller counterparty (not necessarily one with a worse credit rating) could only take delivery of a currency if he had paid the compensating currency amount at the same time, credit and even exact date problems would be overcome to a great extent. The market-maker would only be exposed for the exchange differential instead of the whole amount of the transaction.

General Comments

In summary of the spot date principle, it could be said that the spot date is the second business, open, banking or clearing day after the transaction day, unless there is an intervening holiday in the quoting centre. The only exception to this general rule is the spot day in the quoting centre coinciding with a banking holiday in the country(ies) of the foreign currency(ies). In spite of this exception made for one specific currency (or even several) the spot date would remain the same for all other currencies which could be settled in line with the spot day calendar in the quoting centre.

Precision and care in quoting and exchanging information is vital in all business transactions and in the quick, instant foreign exchange markets it is essential.

Forward Dates

In many forms of money dealing and commodity markets, future contracts fall due on the 30th, 60th, 90th, 120th (etc.) day, always adding another 30 days to the next forward date. There are a number of advantages to this approach, and to dealers used to trading in treasury bills and similar paper instruments, the forward date conventions in the foreign exchange market may appear a little eccentric. However, for better or for worse, the currency markets have adopted the calendar month system for standard maturities. Naturally, the market will also deal for any maturity date for which two parties with opposing interests can be found.

The calendar system is simplicity itself in that if a spot date falls in January, the one month forward maturity must fall in the next calendar month, that is, in February, and the two months' in March and so on. The bare bones of the system appear to be extremely logical, and would not upset the more rational members of the legal profession whenever they draw up loan agreements and find that there is no logical forward date. If all calendar months consisted of 30 days there would be no problem, but what to do when the spot date is 31 January and there are only 28 days in February?

Obviously, the forward maturity dates must observe the spot convention that the settlement day of an exchange contract must coincide with a banking day in the two clearing systems necessary to a currency transaction.

Fixing Normal Forward Maturity Dates

The normal standard forward maturity dates follow a very logical pattern. For the sake of simplicity, let us assume that there are no inconsistencies in the calendar months and that if the spot date holds good the numerically corresponding forward days will also fall on 'good' days. To draw up a calendar with good spot and forward dates would leave too much room for misinterpretation, as apart from Sundays and Saturdays, local and national holidays in the various centres would throw spanners in the works. Furthermore, allowing for the different interpretations of market-maker and user (in another country) would confuse the issue even more.

However, with all the inconsistencies of mathematical impossibility allowed for in that the following schedule could not apply, it will at least illustrate the principle of forward date fixing.

Example 6.2

If the spot date falls on	4 January
then the one month falls on	4 February
two months	4 March
three months	4 April
six months	4 July
nine months	4 October
twelve months	4 January (following year)
two years	4 January (year after)

And other less traded standard forward maturity dates, such as five, seven or eight months, would also fall on the 4th of the appropriate month. Unfortunately, there are seven days in the week and two of these are non-banking days and with forward maturities falling on bank holidays as well, the exact numerical day would not be operative all the way through the calendar month maturity schedule. If the logical forward date does fall on a non-banking day, the spot convention is applied so that the first following business day in both centres then becomes the forward maturity date. Thus, a foreign exchange month could run to 30, 31, 35 or more days and, as we shall see later on (*see* page 73), less than 28 days even if February is not the month of the forward maturity.

To make sure that the principle is fully understood by the readers, let us reiterate that if the one month date, *i.e.* 4 February in the above schedule happens to fall on a non-banking day in one of the centres then the operative date could be the 5th, 6th or whatever. Furthermore, even though the one month maturity may not fall exactly on the numerical day of the month to coincide with the spot date, the other forward maturities can still fall on the 4th if they meet the open day requirement. Consequently, with the spot date on 4 January and the one month date on 6 February, other maturities can fall on the 4th of the appropriate months. Again this practice could produce short and long forward/forward months, and allowance will have to be made for this fact when dealers trade in the forward/forward market.

End of Month Maturities

The end of the month system operating in the foreign exchange and deposit markets is the most contentious dating practice used in negotiating international loans, though users of these markets are gradually becoming accustomed to it.

Following the calendar method, there arises the problem of what to do when the end of month spot date cannot be matched with the same numerical date in a forward month. For instance, if the transaction date is 29 January, the spot date 31 January, then the one month forward cannot fall on a 31st for the very reason that there are only 28 or 29 days in the month of February. The solution to this problem is that, if the last spot date falls on the last business day of a month, the forward dates will match this date by also falling due on the last business day. Thus the spot date 31 January would produce a one month forward date of 28 or 29 February. And if the 28th or 29th fell on non-banking days then the 26th, 27th or the last suitable day would be the last maturity date in that month.

It is rare that end of the month distortions lead to misunderstandings in the professional markets. This is such a technical aspect that the dealers will automatically make adjustments to the maturity and pricing structure. Of course, this method of dealing with the last working day of the month is contrary to the normal next business day principle and that is why newcomers to the money markets find the adjustment system rather quaint.

A further consequence of the end of the month approach is the possibility that the end of the month date in a forward period can represent the effective forward date for several spot dates in succession. This effect is clearly demonstrated in the following schedule:

Example 6.3

Transaction date	Spot date	One month date
24 January	26 January	
25 January	27 January	
26 January	28 January	28 February
27 January	29 January	
28 January	30 January	
29 January	31 January	

For those with a critical mind it should be pointed out that the dates mentioned in the schedule could not all be operative, as one or more spot dates are bound to fall on a Saturday or Sunday. It is just a question of illustrating the principle that a number of transaction and settlement dates towards the end of the month share the same forward date or dates. And in line with the end of the month system, 28 February might have to be replaced with the 27th or 26th or any earlier date meeting the requirement of an open day in both centres. Of course, the same thinking would be applied to other forward months.

There is method and logic in what may appear as madness to outsiders. Why not go forward into the next month? There is no easy explanation. However, practicians know that end of the month markets are subject to liquidity pressures, particularly when they coincide with year or quarter endings. As these liquidity pressures must be reflected in forward exchange rates as a result of abnormal interest rates, to follow the normal next open day method would entail the necessity for the dealers to take two month end adjustments into account in their calculations. Whereas now as long as they deal forward into February they can ignore the 28 February/1 March factor. And once the spot date falls on 1 or 2 February and the dealer deals one month for the first business day in March, he will have to interpret the value of the February/March bridge, but he no longer has to cope with the January/February end. Furthermore, it is much simpler for the dealers to operate in the knowledge that as long as spot dates fall in January the one month forward will also fall in the next calendar month.

It should be pointed out again that the end of the month value dates can produce a quite substantial number of distortions in days in the length of forward months between the various currencies.

Odd Forward Dates

The market vernacular includes a number of expressions that describe 'odd' maturities in the forward market. By 'odd' maturities are meant all the forward value dates that do not form part of the standard forward structure on a particular transaction day. If the standard maturities are those for one, two, three (etc.) months and an enquirer wishes to obtain a quotation for two and a half months he is asking for a price in an 'odd' maturity or an 'odd' date.

Some professional traders make it their business to specialize in odd forward maturities, mostly on a swap basis. They generally charge for this service in their quotations, usually by widening the margin between buying and selling. If they build up a reputation in this field, it is likely that the contrary interests of their clientele will ensure that most of the exposed maturities will be matched in time and amount, showing wider profit margins than standard forward dealings. At least, that would be the outcome in stable markets, but the opposite situation may apply in volatile conditions when operators tend to have the same interests, either all buying or all selling. And then the exposure will have to be lessened by quoting wider and wider prices or simply by refusing to quote for popular, but 'odd' dates.

As a matter of routine, contacting parties should be more precise in indicating the odd date; two and a half months could result in dealings taking place for a non-banking day. It is better to find out the exact date and to request a price for that specific date rather than asking vaguely 'how do you quote the two and a half months?'.

Mistakes in Value Dates

Although the parties to a transaction may have taken every possible precaution, a slip of the tongue or carelessness on the part of one of the contractants can result in a wrong value date being applied to a contract. Most times an error in confirming a forward contract will be noticed by the reconciliation units, and then the offending party can correct the mistake before moneys have passed, without incurring costs. However, it is possible that if the offending party has also entered the transaction in the wrong place on the forward position, he may have engaged in dealing against this non-existing exposure. Sometimes these errors result in losses, but just as many times they may produce profits.

Real problems arise when parties have actually paid and received the currencies on different days. Then it is a matter of establishing which party has been negligent. This is easy when the deal was negotiated over the telex, but when transacted over the telephone, this check does not exist and then the discrepancies will have to be settled, usually by agreeing to share the cost 50–50. Though this market convention ensures that the cost is halved, it is still a most unsatisfactory settlement for one of the contractants who may feel that he was in the right. This type of mistake can lead to the severance of mutually profitable relationships.

When a value date changes during the life-time of a contract, because a 'good' day has become a non-banking day, delicate negotiations may have to take place. This change in the status of a banking day sometimes happens when a government or monetary authority decides, often for very valid reasons, that it is necessary to declare a holiday or to close the banks on that day. It must be said that official bodies at times take arbitrary decisions in total ignorance of what the consequences are for the business world. The problem is usually overcome by extending the settlement to the next open day and, in the case of a last day of the month maturity, to the previous banking day. How to adjust the cost or profit on this extension is a matter of negotiation between the contractants, as there does not seem to be a standard procedure to cope with these changes in value dates.

It is not too bad if these changes only affect the currencies of the parties to an exchange deal, *e.g.* a New York bank buys Swiss francs against US dollars from a Swiss bank. All they have to do is to move the settlement to the next or previous effective day. And, on the whole, when the participants are banks, solutions can be found quite readily. It is a slightly different matter when a commercial organization has contracted to pay dollars to a supplier in New York on a certain day, and has bought these dollars against Swiss francs to be received on the same day from another party and finds that the Swiss francs will only be received the following day. But this dilemma is not really a question of foreign exchange value dates.

Euro-currency Value Dates

Euro-dollars and Euro-currencies follow the same spot and forward convention as the foreign exchange market.

7

THE EURO-MARKETS

History and Development

Unnoticed by most commentators of the time, an international money market in US dollars sprang up during the fifties. Until the early sixties, in real terms, this market in off-shore US dollars was relatively small compared with the financial might of the United States, but was sufficiently large to warrant a separate identity. It was 'christened' the 'Euro-dollar market'. It grew lustily fuelled by fundamental balance of payment disequilibria and consequential currency crises, to reach full maturity in the seventies. No longer a bouncing baby fondly remembered by those who were present at the birth, but now a huge financial King Kong looming over the money markets, creating in its path the havoc of inflation, currency stampedes and panic among the guardians of monetary rectitude.

There are a number of explanations for the birth of this international money market from which the Euro Deutsche Mark, French francs, sterling and other off-shore deposit markets received their impetus. Initially this free market in surplus funds operated mainly in London; at least, London acted as the entrepôt place for Europe and the rest of the world. Of course, the volume was too large to find a home in the UK money supply and the cost would have been too high in comparison with domestic sterling interest rates. Thus, while London accepted deposits on a wholesale basis, they were retailed out to other countries, mainly to banks.

Identical off-shore markets have since been established in other parts of the world. London, although still the largest centre, is no longer the only one. Sometimes the attraction of an off-shore centre is the fact that taxation is low or non-existent, which is a boon for investors who wish to avoid paying tax or sometimes have a need for their investments to be shrouded in secrecy. Without the existence of these off-shore markets it would have been more difficult for foreign exchange activities to expand as they have over the years. Foreign exchange dealers, in order to be able to take views, *i.e.* go short or long of a currency, either have to find funds to cover the shortfall or be able to lay off the assets they have acquired, and the Euro-markets provide this easy pool of liquidity and flexibility. It is a slightly different matter if a speculator has to acquire cover in the country where the currency is under pressure or invest long positions in a country where the currency is appreciating. Monetary authorities in these conditions tend to make these actions too costly in various ways. In this way the international money market was a godsend to the foreign exchange operators, although as always it is a chicken and egg question as to which came first.

As the Euro-dollar market originated in the foreign exchange departments, it became an accepted fact that currency deposits, that is, deposits in currencies other than the national one, became the preserve of the foreign exchange dealers. Over the last few years this development has been taken a stage further. As money is money in whatever shape or form it appears, in many banks the activities of all departments dealing in money, whether the national unit of account or foreign currencies, have been merged under the treasury function. In some banks this new approach has been taken to its extreme and all trading comes under the treasury head, including bullion, government stocks, bills of exchange and so on.

Naturally, foreign currency deposits, especially those created through interest arbitrage operations, existed before the Second World War. However, the market was not as flexible and it was usually a case of an enterprising bank or its dealer finding profitable investment opportunities in another country, often a less developed nation. And sometimes it was possible to invest the money and cover the exchange risk in the 'forwards', still leaving the entrepreneur with a worthwhile profit margin. Thus, interest arbitrage operations were possible and were entered into, but the sheer volume which grew out of the international money market in currency deposits just did not exist.

In any case, before the Second World War the means of communication were much slower and those with speedier access to information from other financial centres and open lines of communication could take advantage of the opportunities when they arose. Quite often this was a question of sending more telegrams and cables to contacts abroad and hoping to recoup the costs by increased trading. The increased use of telex, telephone and visual display units in the seventies has seen to it that vital news is at the disposal of anybody in a position to buy the services or equipment.

Nowadays, it is not so much the lack of information which affects trading, whether in deposits or foreign exchange, but the surfeit of it. There is so much information on offer that the users are frequently not in a position to interpret the wealth of facts and rumours brought to their notice. The abundance of information can result in very active trading, as the participants take views and reverse their decisions constantly. Dealing is now more a question of tactics rather than long-term strategy.

The Effect of Interest Rates on the Euro-markets

Another change which altered the structure of the forward exchange markets was the relative ease with which funds could be borrowed in the Euro- and allied markets and hedged into other ones. The main difference these days is that whereas in the past the domestic money markets, particularly the official discount rate and the treasury bill prices, influenced the forward discounts or premiums, currently it is the effective interest rates set by the international money market that set the pace. Then foreign exchange controls inhibited the free flow of money in or out, or both (this is still true in many countries), which is not the case in the unregulated Euro-market. These controls can cause the external interest rates for a currency to be much higher (or lower) than the rates quoted internally in the domestic market. Obviously a speculative movement against sterling would result in a demand for the currency on a deposit basis to finance the short positions, which, until 23 October 1979, could not be met from United Kingdom sources but had to be obtained outside the country in the external market, or had to be generated through the forward swap mechanism. Either way, whether through swaps or by borrowing, the intense demand would cause the external rates to move away from the parity with its domestic equivalents.

Whether the upward trend is the result of pressures on the forward rates, or the forward rates are affected by the interest rates, is a debatable point. In effect, during a currency crisis, it is the anticipatory activities in the forward exchange market that bring about changes in the interest rate structure for a currency or currencies. This can happen even if the monetary authorities of a country intervene in the market place.

All this assumes, of course, that the operators in a country, or several countries, have a degree of freedom to buy and sell, borrow and lend. In countries with comprehensive exchange controls, there may not be an exchange market in the national currency outside the national borders and then, of course, there is no real effective interest rate, either as the authorities have the situation fully under control, or at least for a time until pressures on the balance of payment and the uncompetitiveness of locally produced goods force a rate adjustment.

The Interest Day Year

The internal, or off-shore markets, adopted most of the mechanical aspects for handling deposits applying at the time in the United States, as at the outset only the US dollar was available in sufficient volume to permit active trading. And even today the US dollar still forms the basis for all currency dealing. As a consequence, the interest year, with some exceptions, among them sterling, is firmly based on the exact number of days over 360 (365/360). This means that if a deposit is placed for an exact calendar year the minimum number of days will be 365 and that the investor will receive an extra five days' interest (being wary, of course, of end of month value dates). On the other hand, the recipient of the funds is in the unfortunate position of having to pay for an extra five days. This may seem unfair to the borrower but is quite acceptable to the beneficiary. Most sterling transactions, however, are treated in the same way the interest year is calculated in the United Kingdom. All in all, the United Kingdom approach seems to be more equitable unless you happen to be a lender.

Why this interest day year, as customary for US dollars, was also adopted for other Euro-currencies but not for sterling and Belgian francs is not clear. And this is in spite of the fact that the interest day year as practised within the national boundaries may even differ from the American or British systems. It is always advisable to check the interest day year that will be applied when trading with a bank resident in the country of the currency. This checking of the interest day year is essential, as deals done in the currency of the borrower or lender may have to be settled under the conventions prevailing in that country, unless terms and conditions are clearly stated from the beginning before the transaction has been finalized.

As explained above (*see* pages 64 – 65), it is also customary to pay interest only on the maturity date of a deposit unless the period is in excess of one year in which case interest is paid on the anniversary of the transaction. These accepted customs rarely have to be clarified when dealing with professionals, although they can lead to bitter acrimony with casual users of the market. It is advisable to state the terms and conditions of Euro-deposit in an unambiguous manner when the other party is not fully versed in the conventions. Euro-dollar loans to commercial borrowers and, in some cases, to banks, will be subject to the specific terms and conditions of the loan agreement and may vary from standard practice in the professional markets, but as long as the loan agreements state these variations in language which cannot be mis-understood all should be well. For example, on a loan, even though the interest is fixed for medium-term periods, the agreement may call for interest to be settled semi-annually or even quarterly.

Value Dates

Other practices in the Euro- and allied markets closely follow those developed over the years in the foreign exchange environment. For instance, the value dates in the international money market are the same as those in the exchange market. Thus, whether borrowing or lending, buying or selling a currency, when dealing with a party resident outside the country of the currency it will be standard practice to deal for spot delivery, unless another value date has been specifically requested. And the forward maturities are the same as those applying in the exchange markets, including the complicated end of month procedure. In theory, if not in practice, all operative forward value dates, including spot, will be the same for foreign exchange deals and deposit transactions. The practice rather than the theory is important, as there have been times that the exchange market for a currency did not permit settlement of outstanding items, although straight deposit transactions could be paid and received.

Calculating the Annual Interest Rate

The simple interest formula is known to everyone connected with the banking and financial system:

$$\text{Interest} = \frac{\text{Principal} \times \text{Rate} \times \text{Tenor (days)}}{360 \times 100}$$

As sterling is one of the currencies using the 365/365 system, the 360 would have to be replaced by 365 for a sterling transaction.

The 365/365 day year approach has a drawback in that it is difficult to compare the interest rate earned on US dollars or Deutsche Marks in the Euro-markets with a similar deposit in sterling, as an adjustment must be made for the five days. This presents no problem if the interested party is lending dollars or Deutsche Marks and borrowing sterling because, at least in theory, he is then receiving more interest than he will have to pay out in view of the five extra days.

Although the same principle will apply, the situation is slightly different when sterling interest rates are lower than those for the other currencies used. At low interest rates the five days' difference has little impact but when interest rates are on a high plateau or the difference between two currencies involved in an interest arbitrage transaction is substantial, the five days will have to be evaluated.

Example 7.1

US$1,000,000 invested for one year at 15 per cent per annum will earn:

$$\frac{\$1,000,000 \times 15 \times 365}{360 \times 100} = \$152,083.33$$

which represents a return of 15.208 per cent per annum when converted to a 365/365 day basis.

An easy way to establish what the effective annual rate is for an interest rate using the 365/360 approach is to multiply the rate by 73 and divide the result by 72. For instance, $15 \times 73 \div 72 = 15.2083$. An even quicker way is to divide the rate by 72 to obtain the extra percentage fraction which will have to be paid or received, *i.e.* $15 \div 72 = 0.2083$ per cent per annum.

As long as the operator only handles in and out transactions, in the same currency, of course, and using the same interest year, there is no problem, but, as shown in Chapter 5 on interest arbitrage the difference in days will also affect transactions when borrowing one currency, hedging into another one and using the proceeds to make investments. The five days' difference will make an impact on the exchange rate for the forward maturity as well as on the interest rate element.

Wholesale Dealing

In Euro-dollar and Euro-currencies, there is a tendency for amounts to be taken and placed on a wholesale basis. That is, a large amount is first taken on deposit and then dished out in smaller lots, though still in fairly substantial amounts, to other parties. The thinking behind this approach is that smaller amounts will command higher rates, as the beneficiaries may not have access to the wholesale market.

This practice can be compared with the functions performed by wholesalers and retailers in the consumer goods industry. Just like the wholesaler the wholesale bank may get the market demand estimate wrong and find that it makes a loss on its selling to the retail banks. The wholesale operator then has to make the decision whether to take an immediate loss or to hedge his bets. With a normal rate distribution longer dates should command higher interest rates than shorter periods. Thus, he could place the funds for longer periods than the original deposit, ensuring a profit on the short end and hoping for the best when his deposit is due for renewal or replacement.

Borrowing short and lending long is quite a normal practice in the Euro-markets. It is rare that profits can be generated any other way. Although, since the advent of interest rates in excess of the old frowned-upon usury rates, the markets no longer show the standard distribution. Frequently short-term periods command higher prices than longer maturities. This kind of market environment may encourage the reverse practice that is, borrowing long and lending short, in other words, becoming more than 100 per cent liquid, assuming the sums lent are repaid in full at the expected time. This change in old customs is a result of the dealers becoming more and more aware of the compound interest factor. The compounding effect can improve or worsen the overall profit by a higher margin than originally was considered ample cover for taking on a credit exposure.

When interest rates are at a low level (these days below 10 per cent per annum) considerations such as compound interest and cash-flow benefits are almost totally ignored. Hope springs eternal for the deposit dealer. He always holds the firm conviction that he will be able to borrow at rates lower than he has lent at and conversely, lend at rates higher than he has borrowed at. In practice, of course, this is not always the case. Many times, gap exposures will have to be opened to manipulate the liquidity position in order to ensure that profits will be made or maximized.

In the wholesale markets it is sometimes possible to match exactly in amount or amounts and dates 'jumbo-sized' deposits and large retail lendings. A bank taking in a deposit of 100 million dollars and then retailing the sum in amounts of more or less than 10 million may find that because of its credit status, it is able to acquire the 100 million at rates well below the interbank market prices. Just as melded rates are essential to check the profitability of large foreign exchange transactions, the same approach has to be adopted when on-lending small amounts.

Example 7.2

If the assumption is made that the bank obtained the 100 million at an all-in rate of 9⅞ per cent per annum, with the general market levels at 10 to 10⅛ per cent per annum, and placed various amounts from 10⅛ per cent per annum downwards, it is vital that either at the end, or at some point in the proceedings, the dealer be able to establish how profitable the venture has turned out to be.

Let us say the amounts were placed as follows:

Amount (in millions)	Per cent per annum	Melded interest rates
2 × 10	at 10⅛	= 20¼
2 × 10	at 10 $^1\!/_{16}$	= 20⅛
2 × 10	at 10	= 20
2 × 10	at 9⅞	= 19¾
1 × 10	at 9 $^{13}\!/_{16}$	= 9 $^{13}\!/_{16}$
1 × 10	at 9¾	= 9¾
100		$\dfrac{99\ ^{11}\!/_{16}}{10} = 9.96875$ per cent per annum

In spite of the high rates obtained on the first tranches, the average rate earned is only marginally over the cost of the deposit, *i.e.* 9.875 per cent per annum. It does not require mathematical genius to see that the gamble paid off. However, the profit margin was negligible. Naturally, it would also be unusual for a position like this to be unwound in such an orderly fashion. The amounts are going to vary and although the market prefers to deal in millions and handy lots of 5 to 10 million, there will be some borrowers who may insist on limiting their own exposure and opt for odd lots of 4 or 13 million. And then it is even more important still to be able to establish the melded rate. In this example it might have been more appropriate for the dealer with the long position to stop placing funds when the rate dipped below 10 per cent per annum. To achieve this he would have had to keep and update the melded rate record after each transaction. This is particularly important when a large number of transactions are involved in unwinding a wholesale taking or placing operation.

In the foregoing example, if translated into a 'real life' situation, the dealer might well have stopped placing deposits once the level broke through 10 per cent per annum. The surplus funds could then have been employed to cover an existing shortfall, especially if this resulted in 'locking in' profits. Or, failing this and assuming that he did not anticipate a steep drop in the prevailing interest rates, he could have used his stock to cover natural demand from commercial customers or correspondent banks. Aggressive offering in the open market, like aggressive bidding, can give the mistaken impression that the lender or borrower has more business to transact and is desperate to 'unload' or 'stock up'. *Similar considerations and computations have to be taken into account when a dealer has invested substantial funds before taking in wholesale deposits to cover the exposure.*

Covering Gap Exposures

The averaging of earnings or costs is a fairly straightforward arithmetical procedure when amounts and maturities match out. Complications arise when a position has to be laid off or covered for different value dates. Then mismatching can open up gap exposures unless previous, mismatched operations are being covered in the process.

As long as the trading volume and the number of transactions are of a modest nature, it is easy to keep track of gaps created and earnings realized. In this situation it is usually possible to estimate the overall result at a glance. Things tend to be more complex when the dealer is a market-maker and must quote 'willy-nilly' competitive rates to most comers, or at least be willing to take deposits at his prices. Obviously, on the investment side, he always will have to exercise greater caution, as placements are governed by internal limits. On the taking side he will have fewer qualms, given that the period between the date of receipt and repayment date allows sufficient time to reconcile the statements of the correspondent bank in the country where the moneys should be received.

It may be unwise to quote for a one day deposit if the inward payment is in a centre in a later time zone and repayment instructions may have to be forwarded before it can be ascertained that the funds were actually received. It can also happen that funds are received but that due to an oversight the recipient bank has forgotten to advise the beneficiary. Banks sometimes stop repayments if they cannot be sure that a deposit was received in the first place. This can have unfortunate repercussions for a smaller depositor, as his status may suffer in the process.

A way around this problem is to pass repayment instructions subject to the deposit having been received the previous day, although this places the onus on the clearing bank in the other centre and is not a practice which should be adopted as a rule; it should be the exception. Unless there are doubts about the status of the depositor the late receipt of funds is just a matter of inconvenience, as this can be rectified either through the clearing banks or between the parties to the transaction.

To return to the problem of establishing average yields and gap exposures, the first and most important aspect the dealer is interested in is the net time-gap between deposits and placements. The effective gap exposure can be measured by calculating the weighted average of the maturity structure, as follows:

Example 7.3

$7,000,000 maturing in 21 days	= $147,000,000
$10,000,000 maturing in 51 days	= $510,000,000
$17,000,000	$657,000,000

As these were deposits the weighted average of deposit liabilities outstanding amounts to $657,000,000 \div 17,000,000 = 38.65$ days. If the dealer had placed these funds for varying maturities in different amounts, the weighted average maturity of the placements could be worked out in the same fashion:

$2,000,000 maturing in 181 days	= $362,000,000
$15,000,000 maturing in 19 days	= $285,000,000
$17,000,000	$647,000,000

$$647,000,000 \div 17,000,000 = 38.06 \text{ days.}$$

In other words, on the 'taking side' the dealer's bank has acquired deposits of US$17,000,000 with an average maturity of 38.65 days, whereas the placements totalling the same amount only show 38.06.

The weighted average approach can gloss over dangerous underlying liquidity exposures. In absolute terms the bank is only at risk for 0.59 of one day (1 representing one day), which is insignificant and, in any case, shows 100 per cent liquidity, as deposit maturities exceed the placement periods. In theory, the position looks very healthy.

The theory only applies if the prevailing tendency is for interest rates to fall in any event, whatever happens, and unless the bank is very small, US$2,000,000 exposed to interest losses is insignificant. But if the total 'book' amounted to $1,700,000,000 or $17,000,000,000 and the respective exposures between the 51 and 181 days were as much as $200,000,000, or $2,000,000,000, then a sharp upturn in the rate structure might have unpleasant consequences on the profitability of the bank concerned. The weighted average check on maturities is really only of practical value in stable markets and is useless when volatile rate conditions exist.

If the above-mentioned lending and borrowing statements represented the sum total of the bank's activities in the Euro-dollar market or for that matter, any other market, the currency being immaterial, the real liquidity exposure would be more accurately depicted in Example 7.4.

To make this example even more explicit, columns describing the average rates for the appropriate maturities can be added netting out to the overall plus or minus yield of the placements and deposits, ignoring the cost or profit of covering the gap exposures. As the month, quarter and year endings can make a dramatic impact on the interest rate structure, it is the usual practice to set out the varying maturities in monthly, or, to be more precise, half-

Example 7.4

	Long (Assets)	Short (Liabilities)	Net	Cumulative
19 days	15 million		+15 million	+15 million
21 days		7 million	−7 million	+8 million
51 days		10 million	−10 million	−2 million
181 days	2 million		+2 million	0
	17 million	17 million	0	

monthly or even weekly, net and cumulative balances. To break down the liquidity exposure further than weekly net exposures makes them too unwieldy for the dealer to have an immediate overview of the underlying availability and interest rate risks.

Liquid or illiquid gap positions over one year are best ignored in the working schedule. These exposures are usually part of a strategic position, for instance, uncovered placements in excess of one year should be considered as having the opposing side in the last cumulative short/long position of the maturity schedule. Possibly a more conservative approach would be one that ignores the opposing future long and short positions, taking the view that this exposure is an immediate one even if the immediate maturity 'slot' does not show an opposing position.

To every rule there must be an exception. If this long placement is for practical purposes protected by a long-term deposit (although this deposit may be of shorter duration) it becomes again a long-term strategic consideration. Long-term strategic liquidity gaps do not necessarily have to be unwound just because the short-term markets show a firmer or weaker trend. If the exposure is very long-term, cyclical factors may bring the illiquid or even liquid position back into profit.

General Comments

The fact that this chapter refers mainly to dealing in the Euro-markets, with particular emphasis on Euro-dollars, does not mean that dealing in deposits in other currencies or in the domestic markets is substantially different. There may be constraints and technicalities which have an impact on the strategic and tactical views taken, but these are a matter of degree. A major bank in its country of domicile may well be conservative when taking on highly illiquid positions which can be covered only by short-term funds, whereas a foreign bank of equal stature established in the same country may have to be more circumspect in its dealings, as availability of short-term funds can be dramatically affected by market contractions. Furthermore, it may not have access to a lender of last resort, such as the central bank.

8

CERTIFICATES OF DEPOSIT

Certificates of deposit have become such a valuable instrument on the international money markets and also in some national ones, that they deserve special treatment. By studying the arithmetic involved in certificate of deposit issuing and dealing, other money market instruments are easier to understand.

Definition

The certificate of deposit, usually referred to as a CD, is one of the few negotiable instruments suitable for trading in foreign exchange dealing rooms. This is primarily because most of the time it is an obligation issued by a first-class bank promising to repay a deposit on a specific day in a particular place. And, as this document is made out to bearer, it can be passed to another holder by selling the paper without the issuer having to be informed of this fact. As long as the CD is presented for repayment on the due date and in the prescribed manner, the issuer is totally uninterested in what happens to the paper during its life-time.

There is some concern about the legal consequences when the paper is stolen and in due course negotiated and presented for payment by an organization with no title to the paper. The picture would get even more complicated if the unscrupulous party which acquired the paper by stealth managed to sell it to another genuine party, and it was the latter holder who eventually presented the CD for payment to the issuer. As in all banking and financial affairs, this aspect of negotiability, especially of a bearer instrument falling into the wrong hands, is not something that can be easily solved. On the whole, it is a question of the operators and investors in the market exercising due care and not being influenced by bargain basement offers unless they have complete confidence in the party offering the paper.

Development of the CD Market

The CD market is organized in two sections which frequently overlap. There are the prime issuers, the banks, and there are the secondary operators, usually investment houses, but sometimes also including banks which find it preferable to hold negotiable paper instead of investing in assets which cannot be realized in a hurry. That is one of the reasons why certificates of deposit command lower rates in normal times than straightforward time deposits placed for identical periods. The issuer provides liquidity to the buyer and this liquidity is invaluable because when the investor needs funds, he can enter the market and sell the paper issued by another party. In other words, he does not have to borrow in his own name. In effect he uses the creditworthiness of the issuer rather than his own.

Certificates of deposit originated in the United States in the early sixties. The First National City Bank of New York was responsible for their introduction and, not surprisingly, the same Bank was the first institution to issue certificates of deposit in the London market. Later on, the practice spread to other money centres and national markets, although the instruments issued there may not be called by the same name and their negotiability is not as clearly established.

With the propensity to establish larger and larger organizations to gain from economies of scale in the early sixties, the need for finance by commercial and official bodies grew out of proportion to the lending capacities of most banks. Apart from obvious constraints, such as legal lending limits and self-imposed restrictions, there was also the practical drawback that a bank in a position to grant a loan based on the creditworthiness of the borrower could find it difficult to raise the deposits required to fund the loan. And, as most banks still relied on retail and wholesale deposits in their own geographical area, large loan demand could not always be met. It was too difficult to increase the deposit base. There was the further limitation that some wholesale depositors were loath to place deposits for longer terms, as they could not predict with certainty at what time in the future they might need liquidity.

The growth of the interbank market in Europe and the Federal Funds market in the United States proved that it was possible to switch funds from one geographical area to another, allowing funds to move from areas where there was surplus liquidity to others with a need for funds. By juggling the availability of funds between the trading banks the risk of a liquidity 'crunch' could be spread among a large number of participants. The different interpretations of liquidity needs and interest rate forecasts also brought a high degree of velocity into the market. Bank A accepted a deposit for one month and placed a deposit with Bank B for two months, and the latter institution lent the funds to another borrower for three months and so on. At one point in such a chain a deposit might well have been used to fund a commercial loan.

Advantages in Using Certificates of Deposit

The limitations of straight interbank deposits for the commercial investor were that few companies were in a position to borrow and lend money at will.

Usually bank lines have to be negotiated and the profit margins that have to be paid on these facilities may take away the incentive to engage in unbalanced deposit activities. That is where the certificate of deposit comes into its own. The commercial depositor, instead of placing a straightforward time deposit, which cannot be recalled, buys the bank paper which only states that the bearer has deposited x amount of dollars (or other currency) at a certain rate and that on a specific date the deposit will be repaid against delivery of the certificate. The commercial depositor is now much better placed to invest surplus funds and to sell and buy the paper issued by the banks to improve his liquidity, and if he has judged the situation correctly, to improve on the yield he would normally have received on his original deposit for a shorter period.

The mechanics, as far as the commercial party is concerned, are fairly straightforward. He has surplus funds which, according to his calculations, should be available for a period of, let us say, three months, but if everything goes to plan, they may well be available for six months. In the old days it would have been unwise for the treasurer of this company to deposit the money for six months, even if he obtained a higher interest rate as a result of this extension, because if during the life-time of the deposit he developed a genuine need for liquidity and his bank lines had been fully utilized, he would have had to go to his bank, 'cap in hand', with the request to allow him to break the deposit. In the latter case, the bank would very likely have charged a penalty fee, because this would have meant that in order to replenish its coffers the bank would have had to enter the market, possibly at an inopportune time. And even if the depositor had informed the bank of his possible need for liquidity sometime in the future, the bank either might have had to include a stiff penalty fee for the withdrawal option, or might well have advised placement for a shorter time.

Before the introduction of certificates of deposit, fixed-time deposits with withdrawal options were not unusual, as interest rates were fairly stable. The situation changed, however, when interest escalated and many banks, which previously were quite prepared to mature deposits before their final date, hesitated to grant the withdrawal option to all comers and limited this facility to the most trustworthy of their depositors. High interest rates and the need for reliable liquidity at crucial times have killed the gentlemanly attitudes of yore. Hard headed business approaches are adopted these days. No wonder that the certificate of deposit provided a near perfect solution for the needs of the depositor and the demands of the banks. From now on, liquidity could be offered, possibly at a cost, but at a cost clearly stated in market prices rather than at the behest of a single bank. To achieve this result there is no longer any need for depositor and deposit-taking institution to go through prolonged negotiations; the parameters are known to everybody.

Certificates of deposit follow the same rules for interest day years and interest calculations as the Euro-deposit market, although in exceptional circumstances, instead of paying a straight interest rate for the period of the investment, a depositor can negotiate the interest to be paid in the form of a discount. This enables the investor to buy a CD with a larger face amount than he could if the interest were payable at maturity. For instance, if he only had US$900,000 he could buy a CD for US$1,000,000 if the maturity date were in one year's time and the rate approximately 10 per cent per annum. Obviously, 10 per cent per annum discounted would command a higher spot price than US$900,000. As a result of the paper being issued at a discount, the bank receives a smaller amount than the face amount of the document, but in effect, this is similar to issuing paper at a normal rate of interest. If anything, paper issued at a discount should be easier to handle in the secondary market than certificates bearing an interest rate, as the secondary market operator does not have to worry about accrued interest and to allow for this fact in his pricing.

A deep secondary market is all important in the organizational set-up of a certificate of deposit market. Without a secondary market – and a developed one with many participants – the paper is no different than a normal fixed-time deposit. Ways can be found around this problem by using the paper as collateral for short-term advances, but this necessitates time-consuming negotiations, unless an ample credit facility had been negotiated from the outset at beneficial rates to the user.

The main certificate of deposit markets only operate in the national currencies. For instance, domestic sterling is handled in the London market and domestic US dollars in the United States money centres, particularly in New York. The exception is the certificate of deposit in Euro-dollars, issued in London by banks established there, including branches of foreign banks. Similar markets are operating in the Far-East and some other money centres, although London has the most developed market in this paper. Attempts have been made to set up certificate of deposit markets in strong currencies, such as the Deutsche Mark and Swiss franc, outside the natural boundaries, but up to now these have been without success, possibly because the monetary authorities in these countries do not wish to encourage the use of their currencies in a reserve role. The introduction of highly negotiable paper, such as certificates of deposit, would make it easier for currency 'speculators' to invest in short-term positions and possibly gain the benefit of lower interest rates, when they ease as a result of large inflows into that currency.

Calculating the Annual Interest

As with most aspects of money dealing, whether in foreign exchange or deposits, maturities of less than one year are easier to handle than those of longer periods. The settlement of annual interest for medium-term deposits creates complications, particularly when interest arbitrage over the exchanges is involved.

For certificates of deposit a straight purchase from a primary issuer either direct or through a broker, is the simplest way of investing in the paper. The interest is calculated at the issuing rate with settlement at maturity or annually if the final maturity date lies several years ahead. However, when the paper is sold to another investor or to the secondary market during the life-time of the certificate, it becomes a more intricate, although basically quite simple, arithmetical operation.

As for most interest and foreign exchange computations, it is preferable to explain the principles by going through the most elementary form of trading or investment and to build a model for more sophisticated operations.

Certificates of Deposit for One Year or Less

Example 8.1

A London bank issues a certificate of deposit for US$1,000,000 for six months (181 days) at a rate of 10 per cent per annum and the certificate is held in portfolio by the investor until maturity. The formula used to calculate the interest payable at maturity is the standard interest equation:

$$\text{Interest} = \frac{\text{Principal} \times \text{Rate} \times \text{Tenor (days)}}{360 \times 100}$$

Or, applied to the hypothetical transaction:

$$\frac{\$1,000,000 \times 10 \times 181}{360 \times 100} = \text{US}\$50,277.78$$

Consequently, at maturity the investor will receive the proceeds made up of the principal, US$1,000,000, plus the interest US$50,277.78 or US$1,050,277.78. On this basis there is no difference between a certificate of deposit or a fixed-time deposit.

However, if the buyer, instead of retaining the paper in portfolio, decided to sell his holding after 90 days, possibly influenced by the fact that interest rates have dropped to 9 per cent per annum and a profit could be realized, the computations get a little more complex. Of course, as a result of realizing his investment, the buyer may apply the proceeds to buy a longer maturity in the hope that yields will come down further still or he may use the opportunity to realize a profit and at the same time improve his liquidity.

Note: An important point to bear in mind is that in most centres certificates of deposit, other than those in the national currency, are traded on a spot basis and that the operative interest rates are quoted for this settlement day. In the above example the investor would have had to decide to unload not later than the 88th day, if this was the appropriate transaction day. Naturally, certificates of deposit can be issued or disposed of for same day or next day value or even for future settlement, but the yields will take these special factors into account and rather than being quoted a firm market rate, the investor, seller or issuer will have to negotiate the terms and conditions.

Assuming that the investor in the example is permitted to dispose of his holding, he can contact a secondary market operator, an investment house or commercial bank providing this service, and ask for a price. The market-maker's price will take into account a number of factors. First of all, what is the market rate at which he will be able to dispose of the paper to another investor or trader? Or is he prepared to hold the paper on book until a buyer comes along or interest rates decrease affording him a larger profit? Whether he is in a position to hold the paper on book will be a matter of having sufficient liquidity, or the ability to raise funds.

An even more important consideration is the quality of the certificate. Who was the issuer and what is his standing in the market place? Even if the issuer is of undoubted credit standing, has he possibly issued more paper than the market can stand, so that buyers may be difficult to find? And though the name and the paper may be perfectly acceptable, the secondary trader will have to check his own inventory to ensure that he has room under his in-house limits. If the in-house limit is full, the dealer may have to dispose of the paper immediately, as otherwise he would be engaging in unauthorized trading. In some secondary houses the dealer may not be permitted to exceed the in-house limit, even temporarily. Similar limit situations also arise with deposit and foreign exchange limits.

But for the purposes of Example 8.1, the seller, issuer or the paper, creditworthiness, limit and market acceptability are all in order. And the secondary operator has agreed to buy the paper in at a rate of 9 per cent per annum. As the paper has earned 10 per cent per annum for the 90 days and will continue to yield 10 per cent until maturity, the equation will have to allow for these factors.

The computation can be split into two separate calculations. In the first place, the parties to the transaction could establish what 10 per cent per annum for 181 days produces at maturity and then discount the principal and interest back to the 90 days by applying the normal discount to yield formula, as follows:

$$\text{Payment} = \frac{\text{Maturity Amount}}{\left[\left(1 + \frac{\text{Rate} \times 181}{365}\right)\right]}$$

Naturally, the formula would have to be adjusted when the interest year is based on the exact number of days over 360. In that case the formula would read as follows:

$$\text{Payment} = \frac{\text{Maturity Amount}}{\left[1 + \left(\frac{\text{Rate} \times \text{Tenor (days)}}{360}\right)\right]}$$

Example 8.2

It has already been established (*see* Example 8.1, page 90) that the interest on US$1,000,000 would amount to US$50,277.78, and the settlement amount if the certificate is acquired after 90 days, *i.e.* the discount to yield equation, would show that the buyer would have to pay:

$$\frac{\$1,050,277.78}{1 + \left[\dfrac{0.09 \times 91}{360}\right]} = US\$1,026,915.45$$

The secondary market operator would have to pay US$1,026,915.45 for the paper. To prove that this is a worthwhile investment earning 9 per cent per annum, all that is necessary is to calculate that the difference between the purchasing price and the original yield represents 9 per cent per annum. This is achieved by applying the normal interest formula:

$$\frac{\$1,026,915.45 \times 9 \times 91}{360 \times 100} = US\$23,362.33$$

By adding the interest amount to the settlement amount (*i.e.* US$1,026,915.45 + US$23,362.33 = US$1,050,277.78), which equals the face amount on the certificate (US$1,000,000 plus the interest at 10 per cent per annum, US$50,277.78 = US$1,050,277.78), US$1,050,277.78 is the settlement the issuing bank will have to make on the 181st day.

In the professional markets the two formulas to arrive at this result have been combined into one:

$$\text{Proceeds of sale} = \text{Nominal amount} \times \left[\frac{36,000 + (R \times \text{Tenor})}{36,000 + (Y \times \text{Days to run})}\right]$$

R = issue rate   Y = yield on sale or purchase

Which produces when applied to this example:

$$\$1,000,000 \left[\frac{36,000 + (10 \times 181)}{36,000 + (\ 9 \times \ \ 91)}\right] = US\$1,026,915.45$$

The primary investor has earned US$26,915.45 over a period of 90 days and, of course, might like to put this amount in percentage per annum terms. To do this he simply uses the following formula:

$$\text{Rate} = \frac{\text{Interest} \times 360 \times 100}{\text{Principal} \times \text{Days to run}}$$

Or, applied to this example:

$$\frac{\$26,915.45 \times 360 \times 100}{\$1,000,000 \times 90} = 10.76618 \text{ per cent per annum}$$

at which rate the seller has earned an extra 0.75 per cent per annum over his original investment rate.

It is the flexible approach and the opportunities to trade in and out of a prime short-term investment that have been mainly responsible for the enormous growth in the volume outstanding and the turnover in the secondary market. It could be argued that, especially in the United States, a deeper market exists in treasury bills, but that would overlook the fact that bank certificates of deposit are issued at higher interest rates and if the buyer holds on to the paper, he earns a better return on his investment.

Naturally, Example 8.2 described a very optimistic scenario. It is rare that investors can realize such windfalls. Normally, profits are more in the 0.0625 to 0.125 per cent per annum range.

Secondary buyers have to take into account that the cost of their purchase is higher (when buying at a premium) than the nominal amount of the certificate, and if they were forced to use the paper as collateral, it is highly unlikely that a lender would be willing to advance more than the face amount. To some extent this consideration also brings into play the greater exposure risk to the secondary buyer, as he has to pay out more than the face amount. If the bank issuing the paper went into bankruptcy very shortly after the purchase, the realized loss would be higher than that which would have been incurred by the original investor, although, in the final analysis, there is nothing much to choose between the two, as the primary investor would, or might, lose on the interest.

The formulas applied to Example 8.2 (*see* page 92) were adjusted for the fact that US dollars earn interest on an exact number of days over 360 basis. In leap years, the exact number of days is of course at least 366.

Certificates of Deposit Issued for Periods of More than One Year

It is customary to settle interest on deposits and equivalent investments at the end of each year and in the international markets this is standard practice. Consequently, when a certificate of deposit has a final maturity past the one year dates, the holder is entitled to receive interest at each anniversary of the issue date of the paper. Certificates of deposit issued for periods longer than one year show the annual interest amounts and anniversary dates on the reverse side. When the interest is due the holder or his agent will have to present the paper to claim the interest and the fact that payment has been or will be made is noted on the document. Thus, a secondary buyer, acquiring the paper after one or more years have passed, can check that interest has been settled on the due dates.

If the certificate is sold during its life-time at the same rate as the issuing price, the calculations necessary to establish the appropriate purchase amount are the same as for those with one year or shorter maturities. The fact that the final maturity date is years ahead has no bearing on the matter, as only the year during which the purchase is made affects the price. At the end of the year, the principal amount and interest rate to be received in the future are strictly in line with the yield that is anticipated. Hence, only the year during which the certificate changes hands will have an accrued interest element, which will have to be allowed for by applying the normal formula, in spite of the fact that the rate on the certificate and yield for days to run are identical. As a matter of fact, the same consideration would apply for certificates with less than one year to run, which are bought or sold at the same yield as the issue price.

Of course, when the yield differs from the issue rate, complications set in, the exception being when the sale takes place during the last year of the life-time of a certificate of deposit. Again, in the latter case, whether the yield is the same or differs from the issue rate, the standard less than one year formula will have to be applied. However, when the certificate has a maturity further than the current year and the yield to maturity differs from the issue price, other factors have to be taken into account. The principle of this operation is as follows:

Example 8.3

A medium-term certificate of deposit was issued for a three year period. The transaction date was 9 February 1980, and the spot date the 11th of the same month, with annual interest payable on 11 February 1981, 1982 and 1983. The face amount on the paper is US$1,000,000 and the issue rate 12 per cent per annum. The primary investor held the certificate until early March 1981 and then sold it for payment on 3 March 1981. This assumes that inflation levels in the United States have abated and in consequence, interest rates have come down to 9 per cent per annum and that is the yield at which a secondary market operator is willing to buy in the paper. (In fact, rates escalated, particularly for the shorter maturities in early 1981, but for the purposes of this example it makes more sense to assume that rates declined.)

In the computations the interest year 11 February 1980 to 11 February 1981 can be ignored, and the fact that 1980 is a leap year does not interfere with the normal mechanism of calculating the purchase price in the secondary market.

From 3 March 1981, until 11 February 1982, 345 days have yet to elapse and from 11 February 1982 until 11 February 1983, 365 days remain outstanding in full.

To find the purchase price it is necessary to start at the end of the transaction and to work backwards, computing first the amounts applicable to the last year. Thus, the full annual interest payable at the issue rate will amount to:

$$\frac{\$1,000,000 \times 365 \times 12}{360 \times 100} = \$121,666.67$$

to which the principal will have to be added: $+ \$1,000,000 = \$1,121.666.67$.

That represents the payment to be received by the holder and paid by the issuer on the final maturity date. With the knowledge of the amount to be received at the end, it is a simple matter of applying the discount formula to establish the principal that must be invested at the beginning, *i.e.* 11 February 1982, to earn 9 per cent per annum to total $\$1,121,666.67$ at the end. However, as it has already been shown (*see* Example 8.2, page 92), the simplified formula combining the discount to yield and simple interest calculation is an easier approach to find out the amount payable at the onset or:

$$\$1,000,000 \left[\frac{36,000 + (12 \times 365)}{36,000 + (9 \times 365)}\right] = \$1,027,873.23$$

It is always advisable to prove the accuracy of a vital calculation by using a different method, *i.e.*:

$$\frac{\$1,027,873.23 \times 9 \times 365}{100 \times 360} = \$93,793.43$$

By adding $\$93,793.43$ to the amount to be invested at the beginning of the year, *i.e.* $\$1,027,873.23$, the computation is checked for accuracy, as the total agrees with the principal and interest to be received from the primary issuer US$\$1,121,666.67$.

Having established the exact amount that has to be available on 11 February 1982, the application of the standard formula will produce the purchase price to be paid on 3 March 1981.

In the second year of the life-time of the certificate, 345 days remain open from the purchase date to 11 February 1982. It is also known that at the end of the running year, that is, on 11 February, $\$1,027,873.23$ should remain after the buyer has collected his interest, but first of all, it is necessary to establish the gross amount again, which is: $\$1,027,873.23 + \$121,666.67 = \$1,149,539.90$. The second stage is a matter of finding the appropriate purchase price on 3 March 1981. This time it is necessary to use the discount to yield formula, as the face amount on the paper is not the same as the amount needed on 11 February 1982. Thus, the amount which will have to be paid over on 3 March to give a yield of 9 per cent per annum amounts to:

$$\frac{\$1,149,539.90}{\left[1 + \left(\dfrac{9 \times 345}{100 \times 360}\right)\right]} = \$1,058,264.58$$

In percentage terms, the difference between the amount paid and the amount needed on 11 February 1982 produces 9 per cent per annum, as $1,058,264.58 deducted from $1,149,539.90 = $91,275.32, and

$$\frac{\$91,275.32 \times 360 \times 100}{1,058,264.58 \times 345} = 9 \text{ per cent per annum}$$

At this point, some confusion could arise as to the accuracy of the calculations. However, when the 12 per cent interest is deducted from $1,058,264.58 + $91,275.32 = $1,149,539.90 the amount left agrees with the sum required in the last year or $1,027,873.23. In other words, the actual interest received will cover the yield required, *i.e.* 9 per cent per annum, as well as the discounted effect of the difference of 12 per cent and 9 per cent per annum during the last year of the life-time of the certificate. In principle, the original investor receives the difference between 12 per cent and 9 per cent for the remaining life-time of the instrument. In reality, he receives slightly less, as the computations allow for the fact that he really should only receive the 3 per cent difference on the anniversary dates, whereas he receives the difference immediately (but duly discounted).

Floating Rate Certificates of Deposit

Over recent years a new type of certificate of deposit has been issued, partly as a result of higher interest rates. This is the floating rate certificate of deposit. The life-time of such a certificate is normally for three to five years and the interest rate fixed every six months for the ensuing six months. This instrument provides an opportunity for investors who are unsure about their medium-term cash-flows to obtain slightly higher rates without incurring an unacceptable interest rate differential exposure. Naturally, if for some reason the particular floating rate certificate of deposit were in abundant supply, or the creditworthiness of the issuing bank slipped a few notches, this could cause the certificate or certificates held by the investors to command a worse price. If this happened at the beginning of the life-time, the loss could still be substantial if they had to be sold to create liquidity. Even though the certificates are frequently issued at a slightly better rate than the normal six months' interbank rate, this may not compensate for changes in the credit status of the issuer.

These certificates will usually be offered at a premium over or a discount below par, and then the buyer will have to allow for the fact that interest will be received on a smaller or larger amount which will receive a higher or lower yield. The premium or discount in the secondary market usually reflects the adjustment between the issue yield and the market yields.

9

OTHER MONEY MARKET INSTRUMENTS

Foreign exchange and interbank deposit dealing do not necessitate credit-worthiness investigations of the same amplitude as those required when making loans to commercial customers. On the whole, the officers responsible for fixing dealing and placement limits have no connections with the trading rooms and may well set limits which are unrealistic under normal dealing conditions. This means that individual limits frequently are too small to be of practical value. On the other hand, as dealing limits incline towards conservatism, the commensurate open risks are small as well. It would seem that it is only common sense that the people setting dealing limits and those using them should not be the same individuals, otherwise the vested interest of the dealer favouring large and ample limits might unduly influence pure credit decisions.

A beneficial side effect of the separation of duties is the fact that as they are not responsible for setting limits, the dealers, once given internal guidelines, can use them to the full without having to worry about the consequences. However, one would hope that if it came to their knowledge that one of their dealing contacts had developed into a credit risk, the dealers would report this fact and dealing would cease until the situation had been properly analysed. Dealers should only be allowed to operate in areas where the credit risk is non-existent or, at the most, minimal.

Thus, many investment opportunities are outside the province of the foreign exchange departments. However, in some banks where the treasury functions are consolidated in one department or division, usually in the same building or even on the same floor of a large edifice, the foreign exchange dealers must also have some expertise in money market instruments that either can be used to invest surplus funds or to generate liquidity. And, in some instances, particular types of investment have to be engaged in to meet regulatory obligations, such as reserve requirements and liquidity ratios. In many countries banks have to hold a percentage of their assets in highly liquid ('near money') non-credit risk instruments which can be realized almost instantly. Normally, these investments include government paper, especially treasury bills, government stocks as well as eligible bills of exchange. Eligible bills of exchange are usually bills which are readily accepted as collateral by the central bank or the major commercial banks of a country. Often eligible bills of exchange are issued to cover a beneficial financial activity for the country concerned, for instance, to finance exports or industrial development.

Bills of Exchange and Treasury Bills

Definition of a Bill of Exchange

A bill of exchange is an order from one person, the drawer, to another, the drawee, instructing the latter to pay on demand or at a determined time, *e.g.* 90 days sight, a sum of money to bearer or to a specified person or organization, the payee. A bill of exchange can be accepted by the drawee who then also becomes the acceptor.

Definition of a Treasury Bill

A treasury bill is a short-term obligation issued by the government of a country, usually through the intermediary of the central bank with maturities ranging from 90 to 180 days, although in some countries longer as well as shorter maturities are not uncommon. The exact terms and conditions governing the issue and encashment of treasury bills vary from country to country and they are not always called by the same name, but, on the whole, whatever their appellation, the basic reasons for their issue and the terms will be roughly the same everywhere.

A Comparison of the Two Bills

Bills of exchange are mostly drawn on banks and accepted by them on behalf of their customers, and as some of these bills carry a favourable status, *e.g.* export bills, bills of exchange, as well as treasury bills, can be very attractive for the banks to hold in portfolio, as they can be sold in the market when liquidity is needed or lodged with the monetary authorities as collateral for short-term loans. In a way, bills of exchange and treasury bills are the first line of defence for a bank in difficulties.

Naturally, investments and negotiable instruments with little credit risk and high liquidity potential do not earn the same yields as more exposed commercial loans. There is always a trade-off between high yield, high risk and low yield, low risk. Most banks, of course, prefer investments somewhere in between these extremes of conservatism and adventurousness in the financial sense. There are also times that there is little demand for commercial loans and consequently, the interbank market may not be actively interested in taking funds, and then paper issued by the government comes into its own. Granted the low return is in itself not very attractive, but the fact that there is little demand from commercial borrowers should cause interest rates to fall in due course and may encourage the banks to place their surplus funds in highly liquid instruments. Naturally, longer-term paper issued by the government then will also be in demand. When interest rates turn down an immediate profit can be realized or, if the rates are believed to stay at a low level, the original rate may still provide a good return on the liabilities employed to fund the government paper held on portfolio.

To some extent treasury bills and bills of exchange are similar kinds of instruments. Whereas the first one is a simple obligation issued by the government, the latter is a similar undertaking by a commercial institution. In principle, bills of exchange are issued to finance trade-related transactions, although there is a tendency to use them as just another vehicle for obtaining short-term working capital. A company in its normal course of business will always have some commercial venture which qualifies for the issuance of bills of exchange.

Commercial Paper

In the United States and Canada another form of financial paper has become very popular and is an important aspect of the money markets. It goes under the name of commercial paper. In Europe attempts to establish a similar market financed with Euro-dollars have had little success, possibly, because the attraction of the cheaper commercial paper market on the other side of the Atlantic has been too great. With the emphasis on reducing or limiting the total amount of bank lending in Europe through control over the money supply, the commercial paper market may become a more viable instrument in due course.

Definition

Commercial paper is in reality a short-term promissory note issued on an unsecured basis by commercial, financial and banking institutions. Maturities range between a matter of a few days to 360 days, although on a weighted average basis the maturities seem to be well below 90 days.

Development

In the United States and Canada secondary markets have been established for more than a hundred years. The real expansion in commercial paper took place in the early sixties when the banks were strapped for liquidity. To expand their activities they developed the certificate of deposit approach, but as the overall cost of purchasing funds continued to increase, commercial borrowers were encouraged to rely more and more on the commercial paper market. Even retail deposits, which in the past had been a cheap source of funds for the banks, became over expensive given the range of services banks had to provide which added to the deposits' cost. In these conditions commercial paper issued by the primary borrower to the primary lender, sometimes through the intermediary of an investment house, was both more flexible and cheaper. Usually, an investment house would stand in between and retail the paper on behalf of the issuer. With their country-wide outlets, the investment houses were better placed than the banks, which were confined to their home states or provinces.

Arbitrage situations between Canada and the United States frequently occur, in which case US dollar-denominated Canadian paper moves to the United States, as Canada seems to have a greater need for finance than the United States. As a matter of fact, the Canadian/American relationship upsets the theory that interest arbitrage should not be possible in a perfect market, in other words, that arbitrageurs would through their actions restore equilibrium as soon as a distortion showed up. The only explanation can be that with fewer profitable outlets in the United States, even though the local Canadian interest rates may be higher, it is still profitable for American investors to buy the Canadian paper. Also, some of the reserve and other requirements imposed on the Canadian banking system may well result in the internal borrowing rates being too high. But, frequently when two countries have strong geographical and economic links, the interest rates in the larger unit will be lower than in the smaller partner, possibly because the larger money supply creates more velocity than in a country with a limited national issue.

General Comments

It would be well-nigh impossible to analyse every type of bill of exchange, commercial paper and treasury bill issued in the countries of the developed world. There are always some wrinkles in the regulations and the terms of issuance which make them slightly different from the same type of paper issued elsewhere, although, in most cases the mechanics tend to be the same. Either the monetary authority auctions treasury bills every week (or at other suitable intervals) or the price is simply fixed and the banks have to acquire the paper to conform with reserve and other requirements. In the latter case, a bank may have to acquire treasury bills whether the price is favourable or not.

Calculating Yield for Negotiable Instruments

The yield for negotiable instruments can vary widely as well. Certificates of deposit tend to be issued on a simple interest basis, whereas other paper is sold on a discount to yield or simple discount basis. For instance, commercial paper is sold mostly on a discount to yield price, while bills of exchange tend to be negotiated at simple discounts. Treasury bills in the secondary market may be traded at a price with the yield having to be established by calculating the percentage value of the difference between the nominal value and the cost in the secondary market. Whatever the system employed, treasury bills will rarely be issued on a simple interest basis. Participants, particularly those unversed in the arithmetic of treasury bill trading, will have to exercise care when buying or selling at a discount.

Straight or Simple Discount

The straight or simple discount formula is a mirror image of the simple interest formula with the difference that interest is added at the end of the life-time and the discount is deducted at the beginning. It goes without saying that a discount produces a higher cost or profit than simple interest with the same numerical value.

The straight or simple discount formula is the same as the simple interest one with the exception that D (discount) stands for R (rate):

$$\frac{\text{Principal} \times \text{D} \times \text{Tenor (days)}}{360 \times 100} = \text{Discount}$$

Obviously, in the United Kingdom or other countries where a different approach to the interest day year is applied, 365 may have to be substituted for 360.

Example 9.1

If an export company in the United States drew a bill for US$1,000,000 on a UK importer and the bill was discounted, the amount the exporter would receive would be the principal minus the discount, or:

$$\frac{\$1,000,000 \times 10 \times 90}{360 \times 100} = \text{US}\$25,000$$

and the amount to be remitted to the beneficiary would be US$975,000. It is easy to see that as the discount is deducted at the time of selling the bill, the actual interest per annum will be higher than the discount rate as:

$$\frac{\$25,000 \times 100 \times 360}{975,000 \times 90} = 10.25641 \text{ per cent per annum}$$

Instead of stating a discount rate of 10 per cent which hides the true per cent per annum cost, the buyer or seller could have negotiated a discount to yield rate of 10.256410 or more likely 10.25 or even 10.26. This would be an easier price to compare with the true interest costs in the deposit and loan markets.

Discount to Yield

Commercial paper is normally issued on a discount to yield basis. This really means that after applying the discount, the net amount earns or costs *x* per cent per annum, which is equal to the discount to yield rate. The main difference between it and straight discount pricing lies in the fact that a straight discount has to be converted to simple interest per annum, whereas discount to yield states the true cost or gain.

The discount to yield formula is slightly more complicated than the straight discount or simple interest equations.

$$\frac{\text{Face value (nominal value)}}{\left[1 + \left(\dfrac{\text{Discount to yield rate} \times \text{Tenor}}{360 \times 100}\right)\right]} = \text{Discounted amount}$$

Or, to put this in a more acceptable form, an amount of US\$1,000,000 discounted at a discount to yield rate of 10 per cent for 90 days at 10 per cent would purchase:

$$\frac{\$1,000,000}{\left[1 + \left(\dfrac{10 \times 90}{360 \times 100}\right)\right]} = \text{US\$975,609.76}$$

To prove that the difference between US\$1,000,000 and US\$975,609.76 represents 10 per cent per annum should by now present no problem, as:

$$\frac{\$24,390.24 \times 360 \times 100}{\$975,609.76 \times 90} = 10 \text{ per cent per annum}$$

As there are no rates mentioned on paper issued at discounts or discounts to yield, and the nominal values of the instruments are plain to see, it is considerably easier to market both in the primary and secondary sectors. The secondary operator does not have to worry about accrued or future interest. He is only concerned about buying or selling at a discount to yield rate which is easy to compare with going interest rates for other forms of investment. Care would have to be exercised when commercial paper is issued or bills of exchange are discounted for periods in excess of one year, because discounts then produce lower returns.

Example 9.2

To illustrate this proposition, let us analyse the example of a borrower who is offered the option to repay US\$1,000,000 in 450 days or can settle the debt now at a straight discount of 10 per cent.

$$\frac{\text{US\$1,000,000} \times 450 \times 10}{360 \times 100} = \text{US\$125,000}$$

In other words, he will be able to redeem his debt for US\$875,000 instead of US\$1,000,000 after 450 days.

If the recipient of this money then decided to reinvest on a simple per cent per annum basis, he would be out of pocket, as:

$$\frac{\text{US\$875,000} \times 10 \times 365}{360 \times 100} = \text{US\$88,715.28}$$

and the principal and interest invested for the remaining 85 days would add a further:

$$\frac{US\$963,715.28 \times 10 \times 85}{360 \times 100} = \$22,754.39$$

bringing the grand total to US$986,469.67.

There is no need to calculate the interest effect on a straight loan, as the point is proven by the fact that there is loss on US$1,000,000 when the straight discount is applied. The borrower would have executed a cost-saving operation, whereas the lender would have lost US$13,530.33 on the overall transaction.

It always pays for those who are not involved daily in discounting operations, particularly when they go beyond the one year maturity, to check the facts and results for accuracy and prove their conclusions by reversing the transaction to verify the outcome.

10

COMPOUND INTEREST

Past Practice

After the Second World War most countries adopted fairly liberal monetary policies to encourage investment and increase production. These liberal economic policies were influenced by the pre-war history of unemployment and the social and political consequences of this phenomenon. Keynesian economics, with its emphasis on demand management caused interest rates to be at a very low level in most countries. As the low interest conditions coincided with relatively small increases in the cost of living during the fifties and early sixties, many money managers lost familiarity with the important concept of compound interest. They became less and less conscious of interest rate dynamics. All was in order as long as interest rates remained below 10 per cent per annum. The fact that the interest amounts due on borrowings had to be paid before the longer-term investments produced an income was of minor importance.

After all, if an entrepreneur invests money for one year and covers this investment by taking out a loan for six months (at which time he will have to pay interest) and he is only charged 5 per cent per annum, he only has to pay out approximately 2.5 per cent in real terms. The effect this early payment of interest has on the return of the investments is: $(2.5 \times 5) \div 2 \div 100 = 0.0625$ per cent per annum.

Thus, the overall interest cost of borrowing short against long would only have amounted to 5 per cent + 0.0625 per cent per annum (based on the assumption that the second half year is also covered at 5 per cent per annum). As interest rates of 5 per cent per annum and lower were *de rigueur* up to the middle sixties, irresponsible money management practices became widespread, especially among the new entrants to the profession. Compound interest and cash-flow were frequently overlooked in financial decisions.

To illustrate what happens when interest rates escalate, it is sufficient to substitute 10 per cent per annum for the 5 per cent. After six months the interest paid will be 5 per cent in real terms, which then has to be carried to the final maturity but will cost the equivalent of: $(5 \times 10) \div 2 \div 100 = 0.25$ per cent per annum. Although the interest rate has only doubled, the 'carrying' cost has quadrupled. Ten per cent rates which seemed high in the sixties have become commonplace in the seventies. And rates of 10 per cent, and at times considerably higher rates, are the norm rather than the exception.

Bad habits that became prevalent during the post-war era included the practice of lending for long periods and borrowing for much shorter time-spans. In particular, dealers active in the growing Euro-markets were forced to adopt these practices, as this was the only way they could generate adequate profits on their wholesale borrowing and lending operations. It made no sense to borrow for six months at 5 per cent per annum and place the money back in the market making only 0.0625 per cent per annum or sometimes less, while, by funding the placement with a deposit for a short period at a lower rate, a clear profit could be made. For instance, if the one month deposit only commanded 4.5 or 4.75 per cent per annum and the deposit could be rolled for one month at a time until the final maturity was reached, 0.5 or 0.25 per cent per annum profit could be generated. This would be the result if the dealer did not expect a major upward movement in the interest rate structure, in which case he would not have engaged in this 'unbanking-like' manner, that is, by prudent banking standards. Apart from the inhibiting factor of a possible rise in the interest rates, dealers did not worry about the impact compounding could make on their earnings. In fact, this aspect was almost totally overlooked.

Furthermore, as most banks engaged in this form of funding and deposit dealing, the effect on cash-flow was significant. To fund 'the book', more and more money had to be raised, but again at operative interest rates of 5 per cent per annum and lower, the cash-flow shortfalls continued to be ignored, even when the rates touched 10 per cent per annum, charging ahead to reach 20 per cent per annum. Senior management responsible for funding operations were, on the whole, more concerned with forecasting future trends rather than studying the mechanics of deposit dealing. It is obvious that when a loan is made at 10 per cent per annum and the funding costs 10.5 per cent per annum that a loss will be made. It is less obvious that profits will be marginal when a loan is priced at 10.5 per cent per annum, and this transaction is covered with a much shorter-term deposit at 10 per cent per annum. However, as the conservative way of running a deposit book, by acquiring funds taken for longer periods than the offsetting of loans, is unprofitable most of the time, it is easy to understand that dealers were tempted to go short rather than long. In the late seventies it even became fashionable to fund six months' and longer positions with a large component of call and overnight deposits on the liability side.

Calculating Compound Interest

As is the case for interest arbitrage transactions, the lack of basic arithmetical knowledge can produce unfortunate results. Most dealers have no problem when it comes to evaluating compound interest for periods of longer than one year. Even without the use of the standard formula the calculations are fairly straightforward, as long as it is a question of a few years. It is merely a matter of calculating interest on interest. For shorter periods than one year it is slightly different and many traders are unsure of how to apply the compound formula.

The compound interest formula is simplicity itself. It states that after one year an investment will be worth:

$$\text{Principal} \left[1 + \left(\frac{\text{Rate}}{100} \right) \right]$$

Example 10.1

Putting the formula in an everyday situation is an easy matter. If £100 is invested for one year at 3 per cent per annum, then after one year it is worth:

$$£100 \left[1 + \frac{(3)}{100} \right] = £100 \times 1.03 = £103$$

If the same sum were invested for three years then the formula would run:

$$£100 \left[1 + \frac{(3)}{100} \right]^3$$

The 1.03 is raised to the power of three, *i.e.* $1.03 \times 1.03 \times 1.03 = 1.092727$. In other words, after three years £100 invested at 3 per cent per annum becomes $100 \times 1.092727 = £109.27$. Of course, the larger the principal, the more important it becomes to apply the correct multiplier. Because a million pounds invested would grow to £1,092,727 after three years and £10,000,000 to £10,927,272.72.

Thus, the compound formula for full years does not present a problem and, as most office calculators these days are equipped with exponentation, (raising to the power) accuracy and speed are practicable at the same time.

Periods of More than One Year

For periods in excess of one year the yield will have to be adjusted to allow for leap years, and furthermore, adjustments will have to be made if the year is not based on an exact number of days over 365. For instance, as the Euro-markets follow the American system of 365/360 the formula would have to read:

$$\text{Principal} \left[1 + \left(\frac{\text{Rate} \times 365}{100 \times 360} \right) \right]^n$$

n = number of years or number of interest periods.

and US$100 earning 3 per cent per annum for three years would become

$$\text{US\$100} \left[1 + \left(\frac{3 \times 365}{360 \times 100} \right) \right]^3 = \text{US\$100} \times 1.094 = \text{US\$109.40}$$

On large amounts the five days' difference will produce a substantial favourable difference over a number of years to the lender, but less so to the borrower.

As for interest arbitrage operations, compound interest assumptions for medium-term periods must be adjusted for taxation and profit distribution. It must not be taken for granted that the whole interest amount is available for investment.

Periods of Less than One Year

Returning to the less than one year problem, it will be necessary to adjust the per annum interest. It is really only a matter of convenience that interest rates are quoted on a per annum basis, and these days, with high interest rates, there is even a tendency to quote on a monthly basis to make borrowing costs look cheaper than they really are. If a sum is borrowed for one year and interest has to be settled every three months, it is a simple matter of dividing the annual rate by four to arrive at the quarterly rate. With an annual interest rate of 3 per cent, the rate factor in the equation would become $3 \div 4 = 0.75$ per cent per quarter. Minor distortions will show up, as three months' periods vary in the number of days they consist of. In the Euro-markets three months could total less than 90 days, especially when the spot date falls close to the end of a month, and at other times, the length of time could be 92 days or more. But, overall, these time lapses will make little difference to the outcome of a transaction if interest rates are below 10 per cent per annum.

It is another matter when rates of 20 per cent and more per annum are commonplace. And, in countries with interest rate structures well above the 20 per cent per annum level, it may be necessary to compute the exact interest and roll-over value of the interest for the whole period before commitment to a transaction. In any case, when high interest rates are the rule rather than the exception, and there is a fairly even distribution over the time-scale, it may be advisable to borrow long and lend short to obtain the benefit of the compounding effect and the consequent favourable cash-flow. If long-term interest rates are considerably higher than the shorter-term ones, this may be difficult to accomplish and value judgements as to the future trend will have to be made.

Fortunately, when interest rates are under pressure, inverse yield curves will be quite common and frequently longer periods will be cheaper, if there is a greater need for immediate liquidity. There is then a tendency for those with liquidity needs to borrow for the shortest possible period in the hope that the situation will improve sooner rather than later. Interest rates may be very volatile in these conditions; they may 'jump' up and down instead of following a steady upward course. It might then be dangerous to cover all liquidity needs in the longer-term market, though it would be wise to average out and include some longer-term funds in the maturity make up of the liabilities.

Example 10.2

The equation for periods of less than one year (*see* Appendix, page 137 for formula) when applied in the Euro-markets will have to be adjusted for the five extra days when interest rates reach a high plateau. This is merely a question of changing the rate factor to include the days element and thus, the 3 ÷ 4 should be modified to read:

$$\frac{3 \times 365}{4 \times 360} = 0.76 \text{ per cent per quarter.}$$

The extra 0.01 earned will contribute very little to the overall result, but when interest levels attain 20 per cent per annum the outcome is more dramatic:

$$\frac{20 \times 365}{4 \times 360} = 5.069444$$

and the hard cash equivalent of 0.069444 per cent for three months on US $10,000,000 equals:

$$\frac{10,000,000 \times 0.069444 \times 90}{100 \times 360} = \$1,736.10$$

Another compounding problem which may confound the uninitiated is that of compounding shorter than one year periods over several years. An investor places money for a period of two years, but will receive interest quarterly. What is his real return?

Example 10.3

The value of every 100 units of the currency invested would grow by:

$$1 + \left[\left(\frac{10}{4 \times 100}\right)\right]^{8} = 1.2184$$

and thus in two years' time 100 units invested at 10 per cent per annum, with interest payable quarterly, will be worth $100 \times 1.2184 = 121.84$.

The principle of compound interest is that whatever the interest period – usually one year in percentage per annum – this rate has to be divided by the number of shorter periods which will be used to settle the borrowing costs or investments yields.

Overnight Borrowing

A popular activity in the Euro-deposit markets is to borrow overnight money to fund longer periods, as overnight rates are quite often considerably lower than rates for, let us say, one year funds. This is particularly popular among banks, who because of their creditworthiness (these are usually the very large banks with world standing) have access to wholesale deposits.

But, even then, no false assumptions should be made. It is not enough to deduct the overnight rate from the annual one to establish the profit margin. In strict arithmetical terms, it is, of course, impossible to fund one year loans with overnight deposits, as intervening weekends (ignoring bank holidays) will produce an average funding period of $365 - 104 = 261, 365/261 = 1.4$ day.

To work out the effect of weekends and holidays over a period of a year and to quantify exactly the effect these have on the compounding of the interest would be slightly tiresome, as naturally, non-banking days at the beginning of the term would have little impact, whereas those at the end of the period would change the compounding effect considerably. There is no easy way round this problem. To some extent it will have to be accepted that weekends and holidays will be spread proportionately over the year and that interest settlements will be made on an even basis.

Example 10.4

Let us assume that for argument's sake, the average interest settlement of overnight borrowing will take place every 1.5 days, then the number of settlements will work out to $365 \div 1.5 = 243$ times. And to put this approach into a contemporary interest rate setting, at a daily interest payment of 17 per cent per annum, the one year compounded rate would amount to:

$$\left[1 + \left(\frac{17}{100 \times 243}\right)\right]^{243} = (1.185234 - 1)\,100 = 18.5234 \text{ per cent per annum}$$

To break even on a one year loan with interest payable at maturity, the per annum rate should be at least 18.5625 per cent per annum, otherwise, the compounded rate would cancel out any profit. And unless a drop in the rate structure were expected within a matter of months, it would pay the borrower to take one year funds, not only because this would cut costs, but also because after six months his lendable funds would have grown by approximately 8.5 per cent.

Financial Futures Markets in Negotiable Instruments

This leads us to the other aspect of the use of interest flows. It is fallacious to take the view that when a longer-term loan is made the short-term interest flows will be invested at the original rate. That kind of mistake is frequently made when loans earn interest during the course of a year, whereas the liabilities against this loan only have to be paid for annually.

However, a development which took place in the United States over the last decade may well assist in solving the problem of investing future cash-flows. The vehicle is the futures markets in negotiable instruments. Through these markets the beneficiary of future positive cash-flows can buy negotiable paper, with the rate fixed in relation to the current market, although the rates on these instruments may be higher or lower, depending on how the market sees future developments. But the futures market is only of real benefit to the net investor or borrower who wishes to acquire or dispose of paper at a future date. It is less appropriate for a trading operation in fixed-time deposits or a funding department, as the constant in- and outflows would be difficult to evaluate in a future context.

Positive cash-flow anticipated at a future date must be invested at a rate which discounts the future; it is better to underestimate future earnings than to be optimistic. It is relatively easy to construct tables which show with a degree of accuracy how interest flows can be invested at a future date based on 'guestimates'. Such tables should cover all the variables: interest rates, periods of yield and periods of investment. For instance, an optimistic view of 17 per cent earnings to be invested in a year's time could show a optimistic potential of 16 per cent per annum, whereas, at the other extreme, a pessimistic opinion could be that only 5 per cent per annum will be earned.

Once these tables have been put together, they are valid for all times, although from time to time additions may be made to reflect highs or lows in interest rates which could not have been anticipated. For instance, if favourable cash-flow has to be invested at a negative interest rate, the investor has to pay another party to accept his deposit. This has happened before.

11

DEALING CONSTRAINTS

Even in the free market countries, there are constraints which impose limitations on foreign exchange and currency deposit activities. Some of these inhibitions are within the province of official bodies, such as the central bank of the country, but many are simply a reflection of the prudent banking philosophies which obtain in most commercial banks.

The official regulations vary between the extremes of completely controlled markets, if these deserve the market nomenclature, to complete freedom in every respect. Even though there may be no official foreign exchange regulations prohibiting the in- or outflow of funds, most countries have banking laws codifying capital or liquidity ratios which have to be observed. In some instances, the need to maintain reserves in the form of primary or secondary reserve assets can make it costly to exceed certain permitted ratios. There are only a few centres left where there is practically no control at all, whether on the liquidity or exchange positions of the banks incorporated in the country or on the off-shore branches of foreign banks allowed to offer banking services. But even then, the monetary authorities may take this liberal attitude simply because they only authorize or accept banks which are known to have well-run operations with self-imposed limits and controls in position, and of undoubted creditworthiness; in other words, the very large banks.

Frequently, monetary authorities fix absolute foreign exposure limits against the national currency, though they leave complete freedom to the operators to speculate in others as long as these speculative activities do not have an impact on the national currency. This was the case in the United Kingdom until late 1979 before exchange controls were suspended. The banks authorized to operate in the United Kingdom were allowed an overall foreign currency to sterling limit, but were not restricted when taking positions between two foreign currencies, let us say 'short' in Deutsche Marks against 'long' in US dollars. Care had to be taken, however, that net currency exposures did not create a currency to sterling position in excess of the authorized limit.

Overall Foreign Exchange Limit

Unless official foreign exchange controls (which in themselves are very restrictive), impose overall limits on dealing, as was the case in the United Kingdom, every bank or organization involved in the exchange markets will set an absolute limit to all foreign currency exposures against the national one. This is a necessary limitation, as the national currency must be considered to be a foreign currency for dealing purposes, apart from providing the unit of account.

Obviously, if a UK bank is short of US$2,000,000 and this represents a long sterling position of £1,000,000, the US dollar/sterling rate is subject to various influences. On the one hand, the US dollar could strengthen in the international markets against all currencies, including sterling or, on the other hand, sterling might weaken against all currencies, thus producing the same result. Thus, in effect, two separate currencies are involved in each transaction and it would be fallacious just to consider sterling as the home currency which cannot be affected by exchange rate movements.

Example 11.1

> If we take the example of a foreign exchange dealing room with an overall limit of £1,000,000 maximum, long or short (obviously a London operation), then the positions taken in other currencies might provide an overall exposure against sterling at the end of the day as follows:

In sterling terms		Sterling
−£100,000	Belgian francs	
+£1,250,000	US dollars	
+£200,000	Swiss francs	−£1,000,000
−£350,000	Deutsche Marks	
+£1,000,000		

> At the end of the day, the operation is up to its maximum authorized short sterling/long currency position. It is always advisable to stay well within the overall foreign exchange limit, as small transactions, revaluations and interest adjustments may accumulate surpluses or shortfalls and produce a position in excess of the permitted amount. In major dealing rooms £1,000,000 would seem a small position and this amount might well have to be multiplied many times to reflect the dealing positions taken in large banks.

Individual Currency Limits

Whereas the overall limit ensures that net long and short positions in the various currencies do not result in excessive exposures against the national currency, most banks will also have separate maximum 'long' or 'short' in-house limits for the major dealing currencies and nominal limits for minor and exotic ones. Limits for minor or exotic currencies are usually sufficient to allow the dealers to take on short-term exposures, so that they are able to quote and transact business in these currencies with commercial customers and correspondent banks.

On the other hand, a bank may allow its dealers to take overnight exposures in Deutsche Marks of DM20,000,000 or DM50,000,000 or more still, and this exposure may be carried into the next day. That is why some organizations call these individual currency limits overnight limits and in effect, the overall foreign exchange limit is also an overnight exposure limit.

Naturally, these overnight limits are further inhibited by the overall limit against the national currency and, unless the managers in charge of setting limits exercise care, they may find that if the individual limits are utilized to their full extent, the overall limit may be exceeded. Of course, the overall limit would be considered a valuable restraining factor in this case.

These individual currency limits are essential, as otherwise, dealers could take currency/currency risks, without these views showing up against the national currency and by the time the real exposure came to the notice of senior management, the underlying position could have turned into a large loss maker.

Most monetary authorities do not impose individual currency limits for the banks operating within their jurisdiction, although many have reporting systems in place that provide sufficient information to enable the officials in charge of supervision and control to identify problem areas, and possibly to give timely warning to a bank that the limits of banking prudency have been exceeded. Unfortunately, very few monetary authorities insist on figures being submitted on a daily basis, often because of the enormous amount of paper work that would have to be processed. Thus, many times the information will only reach them well after the event and frequently the dangerous position already may have been covered. There are no hard and fast rules, but it would seem that central banks which can keep track of persisting offenders may well avoid some of the banking failures due to over trading that occur, fortunately rarely, these days.

Intra-day or Daylight Limits

The overall and individual currency exchange limits are overnight limits; in other words, the maximum amount or amounts a bank is willing to put at risk at a time that the foreign exchange market is closed in the time zone where the bank is established. This means that overall and individual limits will usually be rather small – sufficient, very likely, for the dealers to carry a favourable, or an unfavourable, position until the next day, either in the anticipation of generating larger profits, or just because they 'got caught' at the end of the dealing day. And rather than take an immediate loss they prefer to 'sit' on the position until the following day when the market may come back to equilibrium, or so they fervently hope.

The needs of customers and correspondents during the dealing may be greater than the overall or individual limits allow. To cope with these situations most banks also have intra-day (or daylight) limits to permit wholesale activities to take place. Daylight limits are often set in an arbitrary fashion: × times the overall or individual currency limits based on experience, *i.e.* that these absolute limits are ample to meet most requirements. Although the limit may be sufficiently large to cover one customer's transaction, there should always be 'enough play' to accommodate 'doubling' up. Customer X wishes to transact a certain amount of business either fully or nearly using up the limits, and before this exposure can be covered in the market another client wishes to transact business along the same lines. Of course, if the other customer wishes to do business on the opposite side of the first transaction, this would be perfect, as the second transaction would liquidate the first position or bring it back to reasonable proportions.

As the individual amounts in particular transactions with specific organizations may well be considerably in excess of any established limits, some banks dispense with limits altogether for these special situations. Obviously, the amounts that may be transacted in one 'go' by oil companies and central banks can be very large indeed and, unless the dealer is in a position to take on his book the whole amount, he could find himself badly placed in the market, as news travels fast. If he has the authority to take the order out of the market, especially before the knowledge that the order is in the public domain, he is, of course, in a position to 'massage' the covering transactions by gradually taking up 'natural' offers or bids. 'Natural' offers or bids are those propositions for relatively small amounts at better than market prices, which may be offered to the banks by parties interested in covering exposures at any cost.

Foreign Exchange Dealing Limits for Banks and Commercial Customers

Before the Second World War, and for a considerable period after the War, dealing limits for counterparties were almost unheard of in the European markets. Deciding on who to deal with was usually left to the discretion of the foreign exchange manager and the dealers. For a long time, this practice was quite safe, as there were relatively few bank failures and definitely no major ones, and, in any case, exchange rates for the major currencies could only move between the upper and lower limits of the Bretton Woods rates by a maximum of 1.5 per cent. The possibility of a major banking failure was negligible. Furthermore, as most countries had strict foreign exchange regulations in place, there was little risk that banks could or would exceed rigidly laid down limits, as penalties were severe.

The bank failures, particularly in the seventies, brought this period of benign neglect to an end. Banks began to appreciate that dealers with a vested interest in having numerous and large limits for other banks and organizations were not necessarily the people best placed to make credit decisions. When a leak is discovered, it is normal practice to make sure that no further loss will occur. In the foreign exchange market this sometimes resulted in such unreasonably small limits being imposed that it amounted to turning off the supply completely at the mains. And these conditions applied to all limits. Sometimes they were too small and there were not enough of them. Fortunately, sense prevailed and these days limits are of adequate size and a degree of flexibility in the fixing of credit limits has speeded up the approval processes in most banks.

Foreign exchange limits for individual customers and banks tend to vary in size substantially. As the limit is usually based on the capital multiplied by an appropriate multiplier, in absolute terms a small customer or bank may well get a higher proportionate limit than another larger bank or customer. This can lead to topsy-turvy situations, where the dealers 'willy-nilly' have to deal with names of lesser credit standing just because in absolute terms a billion dollars seems to be more of a credit risk than 10 million for a less acceptable name. Furthermore, smaller names may have to be given larger percentage limits whatever the formula applied, as there are optimum amounts in market dealing. If one million dollars is the minimum amount that is acceptable in the market, it is no good instituting a limit for half a million, as the user may feel slighted if his amount is 'cut back' and may even cease to deal with the market-maker altogether. Sometimes it is easier to explain that there is no limit in place for a contracting party than to disclose that the limit is such that it has no practical value. It is not unusual for this to happen, as often credit officers are not versed in foreign exchange and money dealing and sometimes they are not qualified to judge what is an acceptable credit risk in the money markets.

The approval process can be long-winded, and extremely time-consuming, even for the periodic renewal and revision procedures. Dealers should be aware of this and try to anticipate their future needs. There is also another unfortunate practice that is applied in many banks. If an internal guidance limit is never or rarely used, it has little to recommend its renewal. This really means that a limit, which is only used *in extremis* because the counterparty is either extremely choosy or too costly, could be cancelled at reviewing time and leave the dealer with no 'last resort funk hole'. Again, it will require delicate negotiations on the part of the dealers to keep these fail-safe limits in place, in the hope that they may never have to be used. Banks and organizations which apply 'the limit must be used' philosophy when considering renewal may force their dealers to engage in unauthorized trading with market-makers for whom no limit exists, as the credit risk may seem less fraught with immediate danger than the exchange loss that is certainly incurred otherwise.

Settlement Limits

Apart from the need for individual foreign exchange limits, some banks and supervisory bodies feel that the exposure on any one settlement date with another party should be limited to an acceptable amount, as otherwise, on this crucial day a bank would be too much exposed to default by accident or design. The settlement day or value day of an exchange contract is the day that the principal amount is subject to a 100 per cent loss, if the paying party remits the countervalue in a near time zone and does not receive cover in a later one. Although time zones tend to tilt the balance in favour of one of the parties, settlement risks can be incurred in the same zone as well, for instance, if the clearing bank in the other country or even the same country does not advise the receiving bank that the cover for a sale has not been received in time, or not at all.

Most of the time these settlement defaults are a matter of misunderstandings or transmission oversights. The paying bank or organization indicates the wrong clearing bank in the other country and consequently the funds end up with another bank, or the receiving bank does not know how to apply the funds in the absence of instructions from the beneficiary. The worst that can happen in these circumstances is that the beneficiary is overdrawn and has a claim against the offending party for interest due. Most of the time accidental defaulters will pay up for their mistakes, although when there is some valid excuse for the mistake, such as unclear payment instructions or confusion in the transmission of the payment details, the offending bank may well plead that it was a joint error and that the costs incurred should be shared by both parties. In these days of high interests a mistake of this nature which has taken some time to find out could be extremely costly, even if one of the parties feels that the mistake was not theirs.

Settlement limits do make it difficult for these mistakes to take on gigantic proportions, though for a larger counterparty the absolute exposure amounts may still be huge. Of course, the possibility is there that with a large exposure there will be payments and receipts and that though they may not off-set settlement risks as far as genuine mistakes are concerned, there may well be a limitation of the exchange risk if the amounts cancel each other out for forward contracts still outstanding.

The size of the settlement limit will depend on the interpretation of the real risk by an organization. Some banks and financial institutions are of the opinion that the further the maturity date the smaller the risk of a settlement default, as anything unforeseen happening to a counterparty's ability to meet the terms and conditions of the contract would come to the notice of the exposed bank, hopefully well before the item falls due for settlement. Thus, in some banks generous settlement limits will be set for longer maturities, whereas, in others the immediate future risks are considered negligible and consequently settlement limits for near maturities are larger than for due dates that are further away. But consensus opinion tends to favour the second view that near maturities present less of a settlement risk than deals arranged for some time in the future.

First of all, the actual settlement risk of a distant forward transaction may be greater in that it may not be executed at all. The longer the maturity the greater the chance that the creditworthiness of a company or bank would change for the worse, or that ownership of the counterparty may alter and affect the settlement of the transaction. This can be the case particularly when dealing with countries where a change of regime could result in contracts being cancelled without the innocent party being able to claim reimbursement for exchange or settlement losses. On the other hand, it could be said that if the settlement is sometime ahead in the future, the party left with an invalid contract is in a position to cover the risk in the best, that is, least costly way. Whereas, if this happens to a contract which is in the process of being settled, there is no time left for manoeuvre, the position has to be covered immediately and losses realized. It is rare that the non-fulfilment of a contract by one party benefits the other one. Most of the time contractants are not in a position to meet their obligations because in every respect, whether in normal trading or exchange cover, they have made speculative decisions. Thus, the odds are that if the counterparty defaults altogether, the exposure created will have to be covered at a loss.

As for foreign exchange dealing limits for counterparties, the tendency is for settlement limits to be more liberal for smaller names than for larger ones. Although it may seem illogical in some instances, the settlement limit for a smaller name could total the individual guidance limit for this contact, as any further subdivision would produce amounts which are not of a size to permit dealing in the market place. The larger limits, which are easier to split, tend to be scaled down and to be less generous than those for smaller organizations. It may be unreasonable, but the approach can be defended in that the larger the amount in absolute terms, the greater the pure settlement risk, as opposed to principal risk. And settlement risks, as explained above, can be very costly if blame cannot be attached to one party because of lack of evidence, as dealing is still largely conducted over the telephone.

Consequently, organizations which limit future settlement risk to reasonable amounts and then multiply the amount to cope with the more voluminous spot and short-date dealings seem to have the right approach. They limit outstandings until the maturity date comes nearer the transaction date and then give their dealers greater freedom to operate in the spot and swap markets. A further benefit this practice engenders is that the individual foreign exchange exposure will decrease almost every day, allowing more business to take place, as the majority of outstanding amounts will also run-off in the very near future.

Deposit Placement Limits

Deposit-placing and -taking activities create greater credit risks by their very nature than foreign exchange dealings do. For one thing, whereas the foreign exchange credit risk is really only incurred on the day that settlement should take place, amounts deposited with other banks remain at risk for the duration of the transaction. Consequently, the longer the period of the placement the greater the risk that the depository could go bankrupt or at least not be in a position to repay the loan or deposit on the due date.

It is becoming more acceptable to refer to interbank activities as deposits taken or placed, although some banks still prefer to talk of borrowing and lending and confirm to other parties in these terms. In some countries there are regulatory or taxation constraints which make it advisable to limit loan volume and hence, to consider interbank activities as deposits.

Naturally, the banks and other participants in the deposit markets are aware of the fact that a deposit placed with another bank is just as much at risk as a commercial loan until the funds have been repaid, and this is, in most instances, without the advantages of collateral or other security being provided in cover of the exposure. Furthermore, differences in the rates between placing and taking interbank funds are at best only marginal and there is normally no built-in profit margin added to the cost of funds, as is the case when making a loan to a commercial customer. Thus, the bank, whether intentionally or not, does not build up an actuarial reserve to cope with bad 'deposit placements'. The profits are made on the judicious decisions of the dealers, either as individuals, or under the instruction of senior management, to take deposits at lower rates than they are placed out at eventually or vice versa. In other words, they play the yield curve.

Deposit placement limits are rarely as liberal as those applied in the foreign exchange markets. Usually the foreign exchange limits for banks and other institutions are based on some multiplier applied to the deposit placement limit. The reason for this practice is that once a deposit limit has been approved, normally after stringent analysis of the past results and status of the bank, it is customary to take the view that the individual foreign exchange limit, further restricted by settlement limits, can be considerably larger than the deposit limit.

The basis of in-house placement limits for other banks is normally a percentage of the capital funds plus reserves. Other factors, such as the geographic location, the political stability of the nation in which the bank has its head office, and the country's economic and financial condition all bring their influence to bear on whether a limit is set up in the first place, and how large the limit will or can be. The location, the economic and financial position and the political situation are sometimes quantified in a formula, thus taking some of the initiative out of the hands of the evaluating credit officers. They simply collect financial data on the bank, which allows them to grant a deposit placement limit modified by the other considerations which are frequently collated by officers with responsibility for geographical area rather than credit. It can happen that a bank, which is not considered suitable for a deposit placement limit, may be deemed perfectly all right for a generous in-house foreign exchange line.

Although, generally speaking, deposit placement limits are only set up for creditworthy banks, sometimes similar internal guidance lines are arranged for commercial and financial undertakings without banking status. It happens that some large companies with major national or international ramifications are better credit risks than many banks. And these organizations can command more advantageous rates and prices than can be obtained by some banks. To accommodate these large institutions, dealers are sometimes given the authority to place funds with them at the same, or very near to, interbank rates. These lines are usually referred to as money market lines, and though very similar to interbank placement facilities, they must not be confused with them, as placements with non-banks are loans. This makes quite a difference, as in most countries interbank and commercial lending activities are recorded under different headings of the balance sheet, and frequently reserve requirements and capital ratios are applied to commercial loans, whereas interbank placements may escape these inhibitions altogether.

Deposit placement limits are essential for the efficient operation of an internal or external money market, giving banks flexibility in disposing of surplus funds and obtaining cover for shortfalls without having to issue long-term obligations. As a matter of fact, in many countries where certificates of deposit are issued and traded, the deposit placement limits will also cover certificates issued by other banks and held in portfolio. Thus, dealers are able to acquire negotiable paper issued by another bank instead of placing deposits. Whereas it is customary to use the same placement limit for deposits and certificates alike, it is a different matter when it comes to bankers' acceptances. This is very much a question of how bankers' acceptances are treated for accounting and liquidity purposes in the country where the head office of the bank is situated. And, naturally, the attitudes taken in the home country may have to be modified when a bank has an active branch or subsidiary in another country. Then the regulations prevailing in the latter may well supersede those applied 'back home'.

Deposit placement limits, as pointed out, are essential to permit the efficient operation of an interbank market and sometimes limits can be forced on unwilling reciprocators. Quite often this is a matter of 'if you don't place money with me, I may refuse to place deposits with you', with just a hint of blackmail, even though this kind of moral suasion will be referred to as obtaining 'reciprocity'. Even smaller names in the market context can play the reciprocity game and insist that the larger banks assist them with their longer-term needs. This sharing and allocation of liquidity risks between large and small operators does create an active two-way market, as many times the large operators either tend to make the market move too much in one direction or even cause a contraction in the total volume. The lesser brethren with limited taking or placing potential are not in a position to influence the market unless they form part of a general movement.

General Comments

At the time of writing, there are strong indications that in spite of a general tendency to create free markets in many countries, there is also a contrary movement to inhibit the free flow of funds by demanding higher liquidity from the banks than was customary in the past. Whereas the supervision of banks is a perfectly reasonable thing to expect, the creation of various layers of limits and ratios may inhibit the entrepreneur. On the other hand, they may also help those who have always interpreted rules and regulations in a relatively open manner and have used any gap in these rules for their own profitable ends.

The more rules there are, the more room there is to create openings for liberal interpretation and the more difficult it becomes to supervise and control the system continuously.

12

FINANCIAL FUTURES

Financial futures have made the headlines since they were first introduced on the International Monetary Market (a division of the Chicago Mercantile Exchange) in the early seventies.

Definition

The concept of financial futures is based on the proven futures contracts in commodities and minerals. Any product which can be bought or sold in standardized volume and quality lends itself to being traded on future exchanges. For instance, currently products such as fuel oil and other crude oil derivatives are being traded on some exchanges. And if 'pork bellies' can form the basis of one of the commodity contracts, it can be imagined how much more suitable are given quantities of Deutsche Marks, sterling or, for that matter, treasury bills.

It could be said that with the improvement in communications, it is a retrograde step to have meeting places which are a little reminiscent of the Middle Ages, because trading in future contracts on an exchange is actually conducted on one large floor with stands or 'pits' where specific contracts or products are dealt in, and business can only be carried out when the operators are standing in their appropriate product 'pit'.

Furthermore, the contracts are traded by public outcry and, although this may vary from exchange to exchange, only the pertinent details, such as maturity and rate are recorded for public display. In a busy market individual or small batches of transactions may not even have to be displayed, as the rate structure moves too quickly.

Advantages and Disadvantages of Financial Futures

One of the many objections raised by the interbank dealers to the financial futures concept is that it is an inflexible system. This point has some validity, as exchanges only have a limited number of settlement dates on which outstanding contracts (those not covered by an opposing transaction for the same maturity) have to be delivered and accepted, and naturally, moneys have to be exchanged as well. However, the protagonists of the exchanges would say that when it comes to financial futures it is not so much a question of taking delivery or delivering as of hedging exposures and taking advantage of market distortions. To an extent, the settlement dates can be compared with account days or similar practices on the stock exchanges. The interbank market is more flexible in that any banking or business day can be a settlement day of foreign exchange transactions, or deposits or certificates of deposit. For that reason, the financial futures exchanges will not take over the functions of the normal open market, but will be an addition to the services which these days are required by the financial community. The fact that there are only a limited number of settlement dates, four, six or eight, is one of the main drawbacks and at the same time, one of the strengths of the exchange approach.

As the interbank market, with the exception of end of the month contracts, deals every day for a different forward date in ensuing calendar months, a client who takes a position one day, let us say in the six months, will the following day, if he so wishes, undo the six months for one or more days forward of the original date of his first opposing contract. He could, of course, request the bank to make the settlement date of the reversal match the original maturity date, but that could mean a cost, as the bank dealer would have to adjust his price, and dealing for an 'odd' date would leave a gap, however short. By dealing on the exchange he will deal at a price for that settlement day without having to take gap exposures or having to negotiate rate adjustments. This is as long as the contract is traded, usually up to two days before the settlement.

The main advantage of dealing on a properly instituted exchange is the fact that considerations such as limits, etc., can be overcome to a major extent. The reason is that once a transaction has been negotiated on the floor between two traders authorized to do so, the exchange takes over and stands in between. Thus, the exchange is the supplier (or seller) to every buyer on the floor and the recipient (buyer) to every seller. There are slight differences in the exact constitution and the rules of financial futures exchanges, but, basically, the American, Continental and the proposed exchange in London all apply in rough measure the same kinds of procedures.

The Margin System

The security offered by the exchange taking on the responsibility of clearing outstanding contracts on the appropriate settlement dates is further improved by the margin system. The margin system ensures that any revaluation shortfall is covered by a margin which has to be surrendered before a transaction is executed. For example, a £25,000 contract on the IMM will attract an initial margin of US$1,500 from both buyer and seller unless they previously executed an opposing transaction.

How does the exchange control the margins to guarantee that every loss is covered? This is done in the following way:

Example 12.1

A buyer through a member of the exchange acquires a futures contract for £25,000 for delivery in December (third Wednesday or first following business day) at a rate of US$2: this values the contract at US$50,000. The buyer lodges a margin of US$1,500 with the exchange through his member firm. The exchange revalues the outstanding contracts every night at the closing rate. If that night the value of sterling dropped to US$1.98 and consequently, the buyer would make a loss of US$500, the exchange would in this instance not require an increase in the margin, as there is a secondary level of margin requirement. This is the maintenance margin, in the case of sterling, US$1,000. But, if sterling had depreciated to US$1.95 and the contract had become worth only US$48,750 the buyer would have to remit before the opening the following day US$250 to restore the margin to its maintenance margin of US$1,000.

Conversely, any daily revaluation profit would be remitted to the buyer, subject to maintaining the US$1,000. Thus, the margin system revalues all outstanding contracts daily and adjusts the margin, at the same time paying out profits and covering losses.

It should be pointed out again that is a very elementary description of the workings of the margin system in Chicago and any party interested in becoming a member or trading through a member firm should become familiar with all the operational and legal implications that surround dealing on an exchange. Also, some exchanges may require higher or even lower margins over time and may not be as eager to settle profit margins although all will very likely insist on keeping the protective margin intact.

A further point to be taken into account is that the member firm through whom an organization or individual trades may require a higher initial margin than that stated by the exchange rules to ensure that there will not be a need to call on the customer daily to provide funds to keep the margin intact. This would be particularly onerous in a very volatile market. Depending on the rules of an exchange and the way in which reserves have to be kept, a margin may not be a complete cost factor, as some interest bearing instruments, such as treasury bills, certificates of deposit or even bank guarantees may be acceptable. But this is something which should be verified before entering into a trading relationship with any exchange.

The foreign exchange contract in Chicago was a way for the small speculator to enter the fray, and the number of trades keeps increasing over the years. It would seem however, that because of their lack of settlement flexibility, the foreign exchange futures will not take over from the forward contracts in the interbank markets of the world, although the individual or smaller organizations, which may find it difficult to transact foreign exchange with the banks, will find that they can trade through the exchanges, subject only to justifying their ability to meet the margin requirements. These individuals and organizations are then no longer inhibited by the limit system.

All these drawbacks and advantages and security arrangements provide valid reasons for financial futures in their own right, but there is the added advantage for the smaller operator that with the public outcry system one contract will be handled at the same rate as a much larger batch; it may well be that one contract or a small number will be easier to execute than a larger volume, as the market-maker may limit his dealing price to an amount before he adjusts his price.

Financial Futures in Interest Bearing Instruments

While there are many points in favour of foreign exchange futures, the money markets as a whole will gain more by making use of the financial futures in interest bearing instruments. As was stated in the Preface, financial futures really require a volume to themselves and just the mathematical and technical approaches to interest bearing futures would necessitate several books.

As the range of options as to their use seems limitless, we shall concentrate on those aspects which might not be known and which can serve as an encouragement for the next comer to obtain literature on the subject, enabling him to become familiar with all aspects.

The normal market in financial instruments operates from a near date which may be spot for dollar certificates of deposits or same day for treasury bills or next day for some government stocks. There may well be a wide range of maturities which can be traded, but what is not readily available is a forward/forward market to cover gaps in the liquidity structure, *e.g.* an insurance company or a pension fund which anticipates favourable cash-flow in three or six months' time and would like to protect the yield on these funds, as they expect that interest rates and yields will come down before time. There may be a few market-makers that might commit themselves to selling treasury bills or government stocks for delivery at some time in the future, but as this is not a daily activity, the casual user of this market may find it difficult to locate the appropriate source.

Even more important is the borrower's need to cover an interest exposure to be incurred some time in the future when his loan based on libor or other suitable numeraire is due to be rolled over or incepted. How can he protect his costs that far ahead?

He might be able to if he knew of the existence of an insurance company with a need to invest funds some time in the future, but it is highly unlikely that this insurance company would be prepared to commit itself to cover the borrower's exposure, unless they had made a careful study of his background and creditworthiness. All this researching and studying takes time and 'in the long run', as Keynes said, 'we are all dead'. With a futures exchange in operation, the insurance company's interest and the borrower's needs may well be matched without either party knowing or having to have knowledge of each others' existence.

Futures exchanges tend to operate on the principle that hardly any deliveries take place, that the market is used to hedge and speculate in assets and liabilities which may well be handled more expeditiously by other financial organizations. Expeditiously in the sense that exchange procedures have, by necessity, to adopt standardization, whereas the party with a need to deliver or take delivery may well have to include payment and other pertinent details which cannot be handled by an exchange clearing system, as this would mean undertaking responsibilities for which the exchange is neither equipped nor properly recompensed.

Obviously, an investor with funds available in three, four or six months can actually take delivery of the preferred instrument if this is traded on the exchange. The borrower who wishes to protect his costs is not in that position, as it seems unlikely that in the foreseeable future any exchange will be able to offer the facility to borrow money.

What the exchanges can offer, on the other hand, is to fix the cost of borrowing with some limitations in that it has no way of fixing the cost of funds provided from an outside source. For example, if a borrower anticipated that the cost of funds would escalate by the time he would be in a position to take up a loan or roll over an existing facility, he might cover this interest rate exposure in the future treasury bills. It does not matter what the interest rate on his borrowing is as long as there is a correlation between his borrowing costs and the yield on treasury bills, be they in sterling (when London opens) or in US dollars.

If he wishes to ensure his costs and he has monitored the difference between the yield on treasury bills and the cost of his borrowing varies by 2 per cent per annum or thereabouts, he can, to some extent, ensure that his costs will remain fairly static if he sells a treasury bill or series for treasury bills for various settlement dates. When these contracts come up for delivery or unwinding he can buy them back at a lower price (higher yield) and the difference will compensate for the higher interest rate which he will (or may) have to pay on his borrowing.

Example 12.2

A company has to roll over a loan in three months' time and this date roughly coincides with the future settlement date of a treasury bill future contract. The current yield on the treasury bill rate is 13 per cent per annum and his cost of borrowing 15 per cent per annum. If the borrower outguesses the market and decides that interest rates are going to go up to 17 per cent per annum or possibly more in two or three months' time, he will no doubt decide to sell one or more treasury bill futures for delivery in three months at a price based on 13 per cent per annum. If he was right in his views and yields on treasury bills increase to 15 per cent per annum and borrowing costs to 17 per cent per annum, by the time he has to roll over his loan and deliver his treasury bill or bills he will have saved the 2 per cent per annum and stabilized his costs at 15 per cent per annum. It is evident that it would be too much to expect to achieve this objective with that much precision. But very likely he will be in a position to cut down on his costs substantially.

Correlation studies between treasury bills and other forms of borrowing and lending may well establish that the higher the effective interest rates, the more margin there will be between the yield on treasury bills and interest rates on loans. At a 13 per cent treasury bill rate the effective interest rates for borrowing may well be 15 per cent, whereas at a 15 per cent treasury bill rate, interest rates may nave jumped to 18 per cent per annum. At very low rates this difference may narrow to 0.5 per cent per annum or less. And, of course, the financial futures market may anticipate events in general and unless the borrower outguesses he may be too late.

It is based on these differences tnat the professional traders make their markets and take positions because they have a shrewd inkling from experience of what happens at different levels and where the yields and interest rates should narrow and widen. The application of these correlations can become extremely complicated if, for instance, currency futures are introduced on the scene. To protect US$1,000,000 of loans the treasury bill future may have to exceed $1,300,000. But, as was stated at the outset, the financial futures subject is one which requires investigation in detail on its own and thus falls outside the scope of this book.

Since the introduction of a Euro-dollar contract on the IMM in late 1981 and given LIFFE in London has a similar contract in the proposal stage, cash exposures in the Euro-dollar market can now be hedged with carbon copy financial futures contracts.

In the treatment of financial futures the author has taken the view that a purchase means buying a negotiable instrument at a future date, for example, a treasury bill. Care must, however, be exercised, as the purchase of a Euro-dollar contract involves a prima facie commitment to place a deposit or to accept a cash settlement instead.

13

REVALUATION OF OPEN POSITIONS

The revaluation results of open foreign exchange positions can have dramatic repercussions for the banks and their operators. Normally revaluations are effected monthly. Depending on legal or in-house requirements, profits or losses are or are not entered to the profit and loss account. It is debatable that, as open positions are very much subject to erratic market movements, they should be included in the profit and loss statement only when this is necessary to present a true and fair financial situation to the outside world.

But whatever the accounting philosophy, revaluations are necessary to keep the foreign exchange exposures under control and in ratio with the overall policy stance of the organization. It may be difficult to isolate foreign exchange profits or losses which are fully matched from those that are not, particularly if the amounts and time exposures are only partially or closely matched. If all transactions are matched in time and amounts, a revaluation would not be necessary, as the accounts would represent a true reflection of the profitability or loss on foreign exchange dealing. Even if positions in the forward book are fully matched in time and amount, there is a strong argument in favour of not including these results in the current profit and loss statement, as settlements of differences will take place at a future date. Furthermore, if these matched forward transactions fall due in an ensuing financial year and show large profits (if nothing unforeseen happens), they may well have a negative impact on cash-flow if dividends or profits are remitted. In discounted cash-flow terms a profit which only will be received in five years' time, but is included in the current results, will be a cost factor throughout the life-time of the transaction and, when very high interest rates prevail, could produce an overall loss. It is, however, not the aim of this book to discuss accounting standards and their validity. Our interest lies in pointing out the advantages and pitfalls of different revaluation systems.

Systems of Revaluation

There are several levels of revaluation. There are the accounting standards to be followed which may be contrary to the interests of the dealing team. There is the management revaluation which may be more or less optimistic than the accounting standards, and there is the 'true revaluation' as interpreted by the dealers. When the revaluation only takes place monthly dealers cannot always remember exactly what has happened and they may not be able to evaluate the impact positions and gaps created in previous months have on the current one.

Computerization is gradually solving reporting and evaluation problems, but the results of a revaluation will be only as good as the input and how well the systems analysts and programmers have done their work. Any system which incorporates daily revaluations will be a boon, especially as the dealers may be able to check the accuracy compared with the deals executed the previous day. One hears of different systems of revaluations and little quirks which produce varying results. Even though accounting standards are laid down, operational departments in different organizations interpret the rules in a liberal fashion. But, basically, there are three major approaches which are applied by most banks.

The first approach is to revalue all outstanding items at the extremes of the market rates, as quoted at the close of business on the revaluation day. All forward outstandings are considered to be open exchange positions even though covered in other maturities or spot. Unfortunately, in a dealing room which handles a multitude of currencies, it may be well-nigh impossible to collate all the rates at exactly the same time and in a rapidly moving market distortions will arise. A bank in London which is active in US dollars against Deutsche Marks, but revalues in sterling terms, will have difficulty in getting the timing of obtaining sterling/dollar and sterling/Deutsche Marks rates absolutely right. Consequently, the revaluation may diverge substantially from the truth. Some banks overcome this problem by applying the closing rates as quoted in the quality newspapers, but, as these are usually obtained from obliging banks, they may also differ from the equilibrium rates prevailing at that time.

The second approach is to revalue forward outstandings at their extreme swap premiums or discounts. This is a definite improvement on the first approach. However, this course may not always be acceptable to auditors and controlling bodies, as supervising bodies take the view that *in extremis*, forward outstandings will have to be unwound at rates based on the extremes of the spot quotations, in other words, as open exchange risks. But whatever the accounting standards that have to be observed, for internal purposes the latter system seems to be the fairest way of judging the performance of the dealers.

The third system leaves much to be desired and has for practical purposes been abandoned, as it can lead to a build-up of unrealized profits and losses which are only reflected at a later date. There are variations on this theme, but the following principles are normally operative. When a swap transaction is executed the forward premiums or discounts are amortized in exact proportions over the revaluation periods, whether monthly, quarterly, or even weekly, and when at the end of such a period a revaluation is executed, only the transactions falling due in that period are absorbed in profit and loss or notional accounts. For this method to have any value at all, and to give adequate control, forward outstandings will still have to be revalued, thus necessitating two revaluations.

Apart from these main approaches, there are numerous variations. Some American banks in London, for instance, keep their books in dollar terms, considering sterling as a foreign currency, except for reporting and reserve asset purposes, or to observe UK constraints and requirements. In foreign exchange terms there may be a valid point in using the US dollar as the numeraire for all exchange revaluations, as it is the currency against which most of the international transactions take place. And even when dealing with commercial customers, it provides the base currency for many if not the majority of covering operations in trade and finance.

Revaluing Spot and Nostro Outstandings

The simplest revaluation is that of balances on nostro accounts and positions outstanding for spot or near spot values only. As long as due care is taken in collating the current spot rates, the results of bringing the book values in line with the market will be a fair reflection of the underlying profit and loss situation if realized at these prices.

Example 13.1

Sample spot revaluation using the closing rate method. Bank A has the following long positions in US dollars against sterling: long nostro balance (on own books in debit, on correspondent's books in credit) US$250,000 bought for spot value (long) US$500,000. The nostro balance is the balance of a number of transactions over the preceding month, plus or minus the balance which was revalued at the end of the previous month. The spot dollars were acquired on the last day and bought at a rate of $2.03 to the pound of sterling £246,305.42.

The revaluation would produce the following results if the spot rates for sterling against US dollars were quoted 2.0025–30 at the end of the last day.

Nostro/Spot	Book value	Rate	Revaluation	(Loss)/Profit
US$250,000	(£124,378.11)*	2.0030	£124,812.78	£434.67
US$500,000	(£246,305.42)†	2.0030	£249,625.56	£3,320.14
US$750,000	(£370,683.53)		£374,438.34	£3,754.81

* rate or book 2.01   †rate or book 2.03 (*Note:* the rates at which the positions were revalued the previous month or acquired during the month in question.)

The revaluation of the immediate long position shows that if the dollars were sold at the going market rate a profit of £3,754.81 would be generated.

Whether the volume of transactions and the cost of the use of funds over a period of time would leave a profit margin cannot be established by monthly or periodic revaluations. The spot position may have been carried for a number of months and the cost of carrying this amount in stock may well exceed the profits made on the exchange transactions. Thus, side by side with the revaluation of foreign exchange positions it is absolutely essential that the funds utilized to finance long balances should be costed on an internal allocation basis or against the deposit activities of the dealing room if these are not separated for profit purposes. The use of the 2.0030 rate is justified, as this is the rate at which the market will sell sterling/buy dollars.

Some banks opt for the middle rate in order to show a truer picture for forward positions. In an active dealing room the spot balances may well be negligible compared with the volume of 'forwards'. The minor distortion from the truth will have little effect on the overall outcome.

It would not really matter whether this revaluation were conducted in New York or in London, as the profit or loss figures would be the same, although in New York it would be the sterling balance and spot position that would be revalued and the result would show up in US dollars. The New York bank would make the same profit on its sterling positions as the London bank on the US dollar outstandings, but naturally in dollar terms.

Some Problems of Revaluation

Cross Currency Transactions

Problems arise when cross currency transactions complicate the issue. What happens when a London bank takes a position in US dollars against Deutsche Marks and these positions are outstanding at the end of the month?

Example 13.2

Let's say Bank Y in London sells US$1,000,000 against Deutsche Marks on the day of the revaluation at a rate of 2.3610 for spot settlement. The equilibrium rates between dollars, Deutsche Marks and sterling are the following:

US$/DM	2.3610–2.3620
£/US$	2.0000–2.0005
£/DM	4.7220–(4.725181) 4.7252

Whether the dollars and Deutsche Marks are bought or sold in New York, Frankfurt or London, the banks should produce the same results as long as there are no exchange regulations which inhibit free movement of funds, but the bank which is not established in one of the countries of the currencies in a transaction can be affected by the impact of revaluation in its own national currency.

US dollar revaluation

Amount	Book value	Rate	Revaluation	Profit (Loss)
(US$1,000,000)	£499,875.03*	2.0000	(£500,000)	(£124.97)

(*Note:* it is customary to enter the local currency equivalent of a cross currency transaction based on the same exchange rate, thus showing no loss or profit.)

DM revaluation

Amount	Book value	Rate	Revaluation	Profit (Loss)
DM2,361,000	(£499,875.03)* (countervalue of US$1,000,000)	4.7252	£499,661.39	(£213.64)
				loss £338.61

* book rate 2.0005

A loss of £338.61 shows up when comparing the book entries and their revalued equivalents, simply because the Deutsche Marks have been acquired through dollars. In the revaluation, the view had to be taken that the Deutsche Marks would have to be sold at the worst rate available against sterling and that is 4.7252. The exact rate could have worked out to 4.725181 but the market unfortunately does not quote in those terms. That would have improved the sales value to £499,663.40, an improvement of £2.01.

However, the same position taken by a bank established in the United States would have produced a different result.

DM revaluation

Amount	Book value	Rate	Revaluation	Profit/(Loss)
DM2,361,000	(US$1,000,000)	2.3620	US$999,576.63	(US$423.37)

This loss converted into sterling by buying dollars at the equilibrium rate of 2.0000 amounts to £211.69 only.

There is no ideal solution to this dilemma. Some American banks in London have found an acceptable solution by keeping their books in dollars, thus making it easier to obtain rates, as these are mostly dollars/currency based and do not require subjective calculations. A possible, but more labour-intensive, solution is to have the accounts split into the currencies against which transactions are executed. This would be simpler in that most interbank operations are against US dollars, but it would not overcome the non-dollar element and its revaluation.

The imperfections of a revaluation system can make it well-nigh impossible to identify the currency in which profits are generated and, more important still, the dealer who is responsible for most of the profit. A perfectly sound US$/Deutsche Mark position with profits generated by the Deutsche Mark dealer or section could show reverse results with the profits ending up in, for example, the sterling/dollar book.

A near accurate revaluation of foreign exchange matched and unmatched contracts is absolutely vital to the running and management of an effective dealing room. It is of prime importance that the checking of contracts and confirmations, as well as the reconciliation of nostro accounts is kept up to date. Expense cutting exercises in the areas of accounting, control and reconciliation, unless part and parcel of computerization with built-in safeguards, can be counter-productive.

In any organization with vast turnover in exchange contracts, particularly in the forwards, it may be advisable to have a permanent committee responsible for analysing results and improving on systems and organization.

Forward Transactions

Whereas the revaluation of spot and nostro outstandings is a relatively simple operation, unmatched forward contracts are far more subject to rate and error distortions. A forward contract written up for the wrong date, if of any substance, will show up as a large profit or loss item, although this may not be identifiable without a deal per deal check. This control may well have to be instituted when larger than expected profits or losses show up in the revaluation. Of course, matched forward positions in time and amount will be realized profits as far as the profit and loss account is concerned, although the favourable cash-flow may not occur until much later.

Unrealized profits and losses present interpretation problems in any form of business venture. As an active dealing room builds up an enormous volume of outstanding contracts for forward settlement, it is difficult at the best of times to evaluate at which rates the market will be able to absorb the unmatched positions and even whether there will be a sufficient number of counterparties in the market. For this reason the accounting revaluation should be of a very conservative nature, particularly as profits generated on long-term forwards, even when matched, will produce a negative cash-flow. The dealing revaluation, on the other hand, should be a reflection of the state of the market, otherwise profitable ventures, the consequence of well-thought-out dealing strategies, may show up as loss makers, creating ill-feeling between the dealing team and senior management.

There is merit in the execution of two revaluations, one for public or accounting purposes which is conservative in nature, and the market revaluation, which shows the immediate loss or profit potential. By getting these probably divergent results, it will be easier to decide whether positions should be unwound or run for a period of time. For instance, if the accounting and the market revaluations both show that the profit is substantial, by closing out the most exposed maturities, it may be possible to maximize on the remaining outstandings.

In principle, the forward revaluation is the same as the spot revaluation. The conservative revaluation procedure establishes the current values, based on the extremes of spot, forward or forward/forward rates, whereas the market approach favours the premium or discount approach for appropriate maturities.

Example 13.3

Accounting or conservative revaluation

Amounts	Maturity	£ Equivalent	Rate	Revaluation	Profit/(Loss)
$5,000,000	Spot	(£2,500.000)*	2.0005	£2,499,375.16	(£624.84)
($5,000,000)	1 month	£2,487,562.19†	2.0095	(£2,488,181.14)	(£618.95)
					(£1,243.79)

* Book rate 2.0000 † book rate 2.0100

The assumptions were that the long spot position was revalued at the extreme spot rates 2.0000–2.0005 and the one month maturity at the extreme spot rate, plus the extreme forward rates 95–105 = 2.0095 (2.0000 + 0.0095).

The true swap margins would produce a more realistic result for this relatively insignificant amount:

Rate	Revaluation	Profit/(Loss)
2.0005	£2,499,375.16	(£624.84)
2.0100	(£2,487,562.19)	0
		(£624.84)

The difference in the revaluation loss between extreme and market approaches is simply the 0.0005 variation in the forward rate when applying the extreme spot and forward rates. The fact that the book value and the revaluation result of the forward maturity balance out is purely coincidental. On a small sample of US$1,000,000 a significant difference shows up; when revaluating larger amounts and a great many maturities the spot or forward distortions could reflect the loss of £618.95 100 times or more, and amount to £60,000 plus. It should not be overlooked that revaluations based on extreme spot and forward rates can only increase the theoretical loss or lessen the profit potential of swap transactions. This is probably justified in an accounting context, but definitely not when establishing the worth of a dealing team. During crisis periods this exaggerated loss potential can be magnified further as spot and forward rates widen in response to supply and demand pressures.

The fact that cross currency positions when revalued through a third currency exaggerate loss and minimize profit expectations was sufficiently proven in the spot revaluation, but it should be stressed that forward cross currency positions are even more subject to significant variations from their effective market value.

APPENDIX:

FORMULAS

Simple Interest Formula

$$\frac{\text{Principal} \times \text{Interest rate} \times \text{Tenor (days)}}{360 \text{ or } 365 \times 100} = \text{Interest}$$

Break-even Outright Forward Rate

$$\text{Spot rate} + \left(\frac{\text{Spot rate} \times \text{Interest rate} \times \text{Days}}{360 \text{ or } 365 \times 100}\right) = x$$

$$\text{One unit*} \text{ of valued currency} + \left(\frac{\text{One unit} \times \text{Interest rate} \times \text{Days}}{360 \text{ or } 365 \times 100}\right) = y$$

$$\frac{x =}{y} \text{ Outright forward exchange rate/break-even}$$

*or appropriate amount of units valued by exchange rate.

Cost of Forward Cover Using Outright Forward Rate

$$\frac{\text{Forward margin} \times 365 \times 100}{\text{Outright forward rate} \times \text{Days}} = \text{Approximate forward cost or profit in percentage per annum of swap transaction.}$$

Note: is only close to break-even forward rate when interest rates are at very low levels and interest differentials minimal.

Establishing Percentage Per Annum Cost or Profit of Forward Margin

$$\frac{\dfrac{360}{\text{No. of days}} + \dfrac{\text{Rate for valued or base currency}}{100}}{\text{Spot rate} \times 100} \times \text{Forward premium/discount}$$

= Percentage per annum difference.

Discount to Yield Formula

$$\frac{\text{Maturity amount (future value)}}{\left[1 + \left(\frac{\text{Interest rate}}{100} \times \frac{\text{Tenor (days)}}{360 \text{ or } 365}\right)\right]} = \text{Present value}$$

Present Value of Certificate of Deposit (or Other Equivalent Interest Bearing Instrument with Less than One Year to Maturity)

$$\text{Nominal amount} \left(\frac{36,000 + (\text{Interest rate} \times \text{Tenor})}{36,000 + (\text{Interest rate} \times \text{Days to run})}\right) = \text{Present value}$$

Note: Tenor = original number of days until final maturity.

Formula Establishing Percentage Per Annum of Interest Amount

$$\frac{\text{Interest} \times 360 \text{ or } 365 \times 100}{\text{Principal} \times \text{Days to run}} = \text{Interest rate}$$

Simple Discount

$$\frac{\text{Discount rate} \times \text{Tenor (number of days)} \times \text{Principal}}{360 \text{ or } 365 \times 100} = \text{Discount amount to be deducted from principal to establish present value}$$

Compound Interest

$$\text{Principal} \left[1 + \left(\frac{\text{Interest rate}}{100}\right)\right]^{n} = \text{Compound interest} + \text{Principal}$$

Note: n = number of years of number of interest periods.

Compound Interest on 360 Day Year Basis

$$\text{Principal} \left[1 + \left(\frac{\text{Interest rate} \times 365}{100 \times 360}\right)\right]^{n} = \text{Compound interest for } n \text{ for a number of years} + \text{Principal}$$

Compound Interest Formula for Periods of Less than One Year

$$\text{Principal} \left[1 + \left(\frac{\text{Interest rate} \times \text{Number of days}}{100 \times 360 \text{ or } 365}\right)\right]^{n} = \text{Compound interest} + \text{Principal}$$

IR stands for period interest rate, *e.g.* 15 per cent per annum = $15 \div 2 = 7.5$ per cent for interest payable half-yearly.

BIBLIOGRAPHY

American Bankers' Association: *Foreign Exchange Trading Techniques and Controls*, 1976.

Coninx, Raymond G F: *Foreign Exchange Today*, Woodhead-Faulkner, Cambridge, 1978.

Crump, Norman: *The ABC of the Foreign Exchanges*, Macmillan, London, 1963.

Einzig, Paul: *A Dynamic Theory of Forward Exchange*, Macmillan, London, 1975.

Einzig, Paul: *A History of Foreign Exchange*, Macmillan, London, 1963.

Einzig, Paul: *A Textbook of Foreign Exchange*, Macmillan, London, 1973.

Einzig, Paul: *Foreign Exchange Crises*, Macmillan, London, 1968.

Einzig, Paul: *Leads and Lags*, Macmillan, London, 1968.

Einzig, Paul: *The Case Against Floating Exchanges*, Macmillan, London, 1970.

Evitt, H E: *A Manual of Foreign Exchanges*, Pitman, London, 1971.

Heywood, John: *Foreign Exchange and the Corporate Treasurer*, Adam & Charles Black, London, 1979.

Holgate, H C F: *Exchange Arithmetic*, Macmillan, London, 1973.

Holmes, Alan, and Scholt, Francis H: *The New York Foreign Exchange Market*, New York Federal Reserve Bank, 1965.

Lassen, Richard: *Currency Management*, Woodhead-Faulkner, Cambridge, 1982.

Pick's Currency Yearbook, Pick Publishing Corporation, New York.

Prindl, A R: *Foreign Exchange Risk*, John Wiley & Sons, New York and London, 1976.

Swiss Bank Corporation: *Foreign Exchange*, 1973.

Wainman, David: *Currency Fluctuation: Accounting and Taxation Implications*, Woodhead-Faulkner, Cambridge, 1976.

Weisweiller, Rudi: *Foreign Exchange*, George Allen & Unwin, London, 1972.

INDEX